Into the Heart

A Journey through the Theology of the Body

An Adult Faith Formation Program

Presented by
CHRISTOPHER WEST

The **gift**

free. total. faithful. fruitful.

STUDENT WORKBOOK

ABBREVIATIONS

CCC   *Catechism of the Catholic Church*, Second Edition (Libreria Editrice Vaticana, 1997)

CTH   *Crossing the Threshold of Hope*, John Paul II (Knopf, 1994)

DC   *Deus Caritas Est*, Benedict XVI's Encyclical Letter *God is Love* (Pauline, 2006)

DV   *Dominum et Vivificantem*, John Paul II's Encyclical Letter on the Holy Spirit (Pauline, 1986)

EV   *Evangelium Vitae*, John Paul II's Encyclical Letter on the Gospel of Life (Pauline, 1995)

FC   *Familiaris Consortio*, John Paul II's Apostolic Exhortation on the Christian Family (Pauline, 1981)

GS   *Gaudium et Spes*, Vatican II's Pastoral Constitution on the Church in the Modern World (Pauline, 1965)

LF   *Letter to Families*, John Paul II's Letter in the Year of the Family (Pauline, 1994)

LR   *Love and Responsibility*, Karol Wojtyla's (John Paul II's) philosophical work on sexuality (Ignatius, 1993)

MD   *Mulieris Dignitatem*, John Paul II's Apostolic Letter on the Dignity and Vocation of Women (Pauline, 1988)

MI   *Memory and Identity*, John Paul II's final written work before his death (Rizzoli, 2005).

NMI   *Novo Millennio Ineunte*, John Paul II's Apostolic Letter at the Close of the Great Jubilee (Pauline, 2001)

PC   *Person and Community: Selected Essays* (of Karol Wojtyla's), trans. Theresa Sandok (Peter Lang, 1993)

RC   *Redemptoris Custos*, John Paul II's Apostolic Exhortation on Saint Joseph (Pauline, 1989)

RH   *Redemptor Hominis*, John Paul II's Encyclical Letter on the Redeemer of Man (Pauline, 1979)

RW   *Rise, Let us Be on Our Way*, John Paul II's book reflecting on his life as a bishop (Warner Books, 2004)

SS   *Spe Salvi*, Pope Benedict XVI's encyclical letter *On Christian Hope* (Pauline, 2007)

TOB   *Man and Woman He Created Them: A Theology of the Body*, John Paul II's general audience addresses on Human Love in the Divine Plan (Pauline, 2006)

TT   *Theotokos*, John Paul II's Wednesday Catecheses on Mary, Mother of God (Pauline, 2000)

VS   *Veritatis Splendor*, John Paul II's Encyclical Letter on the Splendor of Truth (Pauline, 1993)

WH   *Witness to Hope*, George Weigel's biography of Pope John Paul II (Harper Collins, 1999)

Nihil obstat: Rev. J. Brian Bransfield, S.T.D.
            Censor Librorum
            September 9, 2008

Imprimatur: +Justin Cardinal Rigali
            Archbishop of Philadelphia
            September 11, 2008

All Scripture quotations contained herein are from the Revised Standard Version of the Bible–Catholic Edition, copyright © 1965, 1966 by the Division of Christian Education of the National Council of Churches of Christ in the United States of America.

Published by Ascension Press
Post Office Box 1990
West Chester, PA 19380
Orders: 1-800-376-0520
www.AscensionPress.com

Cover design by Devin Schadt

Printed in the United States of America

ISBN 978-1-934217-44-3

CONTENTS

The Gift is a dynamic study series based on Pope John Paul II's revolutionary teaching of the Theology of the Body. Written and presented by Christopher West, The Gift is a comprehensive system designed to lay a firm foundation for individuals, groups and parishes desiring to learn and integrate the Theology of the Body into their lives. The Gift is a bold, new study that incorporates a completely updated translation of John Paul II's original text, along with the "hidden" talks he never delivered – only recently discovered in the Vatican archives.

Into the Heart: A Journey Through the Theology of the Body, is a 16-part, 8-hour presentation that moves you deeper into the rich catechesis of the Theology of the Body. You will receive the tools necessary to develop the sacramental worldview that is so crucial to living an authentic human sexuality.

JOURNEY INTO THE Heart

Session 1

A VISION OF HOPE FOR THE HEART

1. REVIEW OF PREVIOUS SERIES

Key points from Session One: *"An Education in Being Human"*

- The Theology of the Body (TOB) is not merely a reflection on marriage. Rather, the TOB provides a "lens" through which to view the whole mystery of human life.

- The human person is not a "spirit" trapped in a body, but rather a profound *unity* of body and soul. The human body expresses the mystery of the human person.

- In the *Incarnation*, God has chosen to reveal himself in and through human flesh – theology *of the body*. This phrase represents the very logic of Christianity.

- The thesis of the TOB is that the body alone is capable of making visible what is invisible – the spiritual and divine. God created the human body to be a sign of the mystery hidden within the Trinity for all eternity.

2. INTO THE HEART

What Is the "Heart"?

The "heart" is our deepest interior self where we are "alone" with ourselves and with God.

- The heart is where we experience the forces of good and evil competing against each other. Hence, it's where we know and experience the true meaning of the body, or, because of the hardness of our hearts, fail to do so.

- Using a physical reality such as the "heart" (a muscle in our chests) to speak of a deep, interior, spiritual reality confirms the basic principle of the TOB: the body reveals profound spiritual mysteries.

    2a. "The heart is our hidden center, beyond the grasp of our reason and of others; only the Spirit of God can fathom the human heart and know it fully. The heart is the place of decision, deeper than our psychic drives. It is the place of truth, where we choose life or death. It is the place of encounter, because as image of God we live in relation" (CCC 2563).

Wounded Hearts in Need of Healing

In his TOB, John Paul II immediately focuses our attention on Christ's words about the human heart – its woundedness and its need for healing: "For your hardness of heart Moses allowed you to divorce your wives, but from the beginning it was not so" (Mt 19:8).

- A prayerful study of the TOB is not only "informational" but also "transformational."

- We should seek not only to open our *minds* to the intellectual riches of John Paul II's teaching, but also our *hearts* to its life-changing power.

2b. "I always tried to achieve a harmony between faith, reason, and the heart. These are profoundly connected, each giving life to the other. This coming together of faith, reason, and the heart is strongly influenced by our sense of wonder at the miracle of a human person – at man's likeness to the Triune God, at the immensely profound bond between love and truth, at the mystery of mutual self-giving and the life that it generates" (RW, p. 97).

2c. "Saint Augustine … defines prayer as an exercise of desire. Man was created for greatness – for God himself; he was created to be filled by God. But his heart is too small for the greatness to which it is destined. It must be stretched. 'By delaying [his gift], God strengthens our desire; through desire he enlarges our soul and by expanding it he increases its capacity [for receiving him]'" (Benedict XVI, SS 33).

2d. "'Suppose that God wishes to fill you with honey; but if you are full of vinegar, where will you put the honey?' The vessel, that is your heart, must first be enlarged and then cleansed, freed from the vinegar and its taste. This requires hard work and is painful, but in this way alone do we become suited to that for which we are destined" (Benedict XVI, SS 33).

2e. "Man cannot live without love. He remains a being that is incomprehensible for himself, his life is senseless, if love is not *revealed to him*, if he does not *encounter* love, if he does not *experience* it and *make it his own*, if he does not *participate intimately* in it … The man who wishes to understand himself thoroughly must with his *unrest*, *uncertainty* and even *his weakness and sinfulness*, with his life and death, *draw near to Christ*. He must, so to speak, *enter into him* with all his own self, he must '*appropriate*' and *assimilate* the whole reality of the Incarnation and Redemption in order to find himself. If that profound process takes place within him, he then bears fruit not only of adoration of God but also of deep wonder at himself … In reality, the name for that deep amazement at man's worth and dignity is the Gospel, that is to say: the Good News. It is also called Christianity" (RH 10, emphasis added).

"THE CHOICE YOU FACE CONSTANTLY IS WHETHER YOU ARE TAKING YOUR WOUNDS TO YOUR HEAD OR YOUR HEART. IN YOUR HEAD YOU CAN ANALYZE THEM, FIND THEIR CAUSES AND CONSEQUENCES, AND COIN WORDS TO SPEAK AND WRITE ABOUT THEM. BUT NO FINAL HEALING IS LIKELY TO COME FROM THAT SOURCE. YOU NEED TO LET YOUR WOUNDS GO DOWN TO YOUR HEART. THEN YOU CAN LIVE THROUGH THEM AND DISCOVER THAT THEY WILL NOT DESTROY YOU."

– HENRI NOUWEN

When *Humanae Vitae* was released, the secular media predicted that the papacy may well topple under the weight of so glaring a blunder. Paul VI predicted that if the teaching were ignored, marriage and the family may well topple under the weight of its error. Society, he said, would experience the breakdown of the family, the lowering of morality, increase in disrespect for women, government imposition on the family, and scientific domination of human life in other areas. Who was right?

3. ORIGIN AND STRUCTURE OF THE TEACHING

Response to the *Humanae Vitae* Crisis

The TOB originated in response to something Pope Paul VI said in his much contested encyclical *Humanae Vitae* (*Of Human Life*):

> **3a.** "The problem of birth [regulation], like every other problem regarding human life, is to be considered beyond partial perspectives." It must be seen "in light of a total vision of man and of his vocation, not only his natural and earthly, but also his supernatural and eternal vocation" (HV 7).

Paul VI, however, did not provide us with an extensive articulation of this 'total vision of man and his vocation. John Paul II does, and that, essentially, is what his TOB is.

- The TOB is the presentation of what John Paul II calls an "adequate anthropology" (anthropology is the "study of man," the study of what it means to be human).

- "Adequate" does not mean "that will do," but "full" and "complete." In turn, this full and complete vision of man provides the basis for understanding the human being's vocation to love as God loves.

- Only in this light can we understand the controversial, yet *essential*, teaching of *Humanae Vitae*.

> **3b.** The whole of the TOB constitutes *"an extensive commentary* on the doctrine contained precisely in *Humanae Vitae"* (TOB 133:2). For questions spring from *Humanae Vitae* "that run in some way through the whole of our reflections … This is important from the point of view of structure and method" (TOB 133:4).

Being Human: An "Adequate Anthropology"

In short, in order to provide a thorough response to the "*Humanae Vitae* crisis," the TOB seeks to answer two of the most fundamental human questions:

(1) *What does it mean to be human*? ("adequate anthropology")

(2) *How do I live my life in a way that will bring true happiness*? (vocation and ethics)

The following is an effective way of presenting the structure of the teaching:

Part I: Establishing an "Adequate Anthropology"

- Our Origin
- Our History
- Our Destiny

Part II: Applying an "Adequate Anthropology"

- Christian Celibacy
- Christian Marriage
- *Humanae Vitae*

John Paul II's original manuscript divides the text in the following manner:

Part I: The Words of Christ

- Christ Appeals to the "Beginning"
- Christ Appeals to the Human Heart
- Christ Appeals to the Resurrection
  – Celibacy for the Kingdom

Part II: The Sacrament

- The Dimension of Covenant and of Grace
- The Dimension of the Sign
- He Gave Them the Law of Life as Their Inheritance

> 3c. "One must immediately observe, in fact, that the term 'theology of the body' goes far beyond the content of the reflections presented here. These reflections do not include many problems belonging … to the theology of the body (e.g., the problem of suffering and death, so important in the biblical message). One must say this clearly" (TOB 133:1).

- The "heart" is our deepest interior self where we are "alone" with ourselves and with God. In TOB, John Paul II immediately focuses our attention on Christ's words about the human heart – its woundedness and its need for healing.

- A prayerful study of TOB is not only "informational" but also "transformational." We should seek not only to open our *minds* to the intellectual riches of John Paul II's teaching, but also our *hearts* to its life-changing power.

- In short, in order to provide a thorough response to the "*Humanae Vitae* crisis," TOB seeks to answer two of the most fundamental human questions:

  (1) *What does it mean to be human*? ("adequate anthropology")

  (2) *How do I live my life in a way that will bring true happiness*? (vocation and ethics)

STUDY QUESTIONS FOR:

SESSION 1: A VISION OF HOPE FOR THE HEART

1. John Paul II's TOB provides great intellectual treasures that theologians will be studying and unpacking for centuries. What is the danger, however, of keeping this teaching "in the head" and not allowing it to penetrate "into the heart"?

2. Were you alive when the encyclical *Humanae Vitae* was published? If so, what do you remember about the controversy that followed?

3. How was the teaching of *Humanae Vitae* presented to you growing up? Was it presented at all?

4. Why is it necessary to view the teaching of the Church on the immorality of contraception in light of a total vision of man and his vocation?

5. Without quoting John Paul II or Christopher West, how would you answer the question *What does it mean to be human*?

6. Again, without quoting John Paul II or Christopher West, how would you answer the question *How do I live my life in a way that will bring true happiness*?

Session 2

"NUPTIAL UNION": A CALL TO
DEEP INTIMACY WITH GOD

1. REVIEW OF PREVIOUS SERIES

Key points from Session Two: *"The Great Analogy of Spousal Love"*

- The human body whispers the innermost secret of God – that God himself is an eternal exchange of life-giving love, and that we are destined to share in that life and love as male and female.

- The one-flesh union of man and woman in Genesis points right from the beginning to the eternal union of Christ and the Church in the book of Revelation. These bookends of the Bible reveal that God's eternal plan is to "marry" us and to fill his Bride with eternal life.

- Christianity cannot be properly understood unless we properly understand our creation as male and female and the call of the two to become "one flesh." This is why the enemy seeks to distort sexuality – to keep us from the truth of Christ and the Church.

2. THE MYSTICAL MARRIAGE

Influence of Saint John of the Cross

Michael Waldstein observes that the young Karol Wojtyla gained a threefold conviction from studying St. John of the Cross that he carried with him throughout his life as priest, bishop, cardinal, and pope (see TOB, pp. 23-24, 29-34, 78).

1. Love involves the gift of self (recall the "spousal meaning of the body").

2. The relationship of spouses is the paradigm of self-giving love in human experience.

3. The relationship of Father, Son, and Holy Spirit is the source and model of all self-giving love.

2a. When Christ "prayed to the Father 'that all may be one … as we are one' (Jn 17:21-22), he opened up vistas closed to human reason, for he implied a certain likeness between the union of divine Persons, and the unity of God's children in truth and love. It follows then, that if man is the only creature on earth that God willed for its own sake, man can only find himself through the sincere gift of self" (GS 24).

2b. "According to St. John of the Cross, the marriage analogy is appropriate across the whole breadth of Christian experience … It is most applicable, however, to what St. John of the Cross calls 'spiritual marriage,' which follows 'spiritual betrothal' … The defining element of 'spiritual marriage' … is the total surrendering of the self-possession of each to the other, analogous to the consummation of love by sexual union in marriage" (Waldstein, TOB, p. 30-31).

2c. "The personal relation of the Son to the Father is something that man cannot conceive of nor the angelic powers even dimly see: and yet, the Spirit of the Son grants a participation in that very relation to us who believe that Jesus is the Christ and that we are born of God" (CCC 2780).

We're All Called to Be "Mystics"

The mystical life is not only for "super" Christians. To live a "mystical life" is the *normal* Christian life. Each of us is called to be an "every day mystic."

- To be a "mystic" means to live all of life from "within" the *great mystery* of Christ's spousal union with the Church – to be taken up by it, to be aflame with divine love.

- Mystics are men and women who – through all of life's joys and trials – fall ever more deeply in love with God because of an ever-growing awareness of God's burning love for them.

- Far from being disconnected from reality, mystics are those who see all of reality *as it truly is*. They come to an ever clearer vision of God in all things and all things in God. They see God's plan for man and the universe unfolding all around them and abandon themselves to it with loving trust.

2d. "Against those who dismiss St. John of the Cross as preoccupied with extraordinary and miraculous mystical phenomena that are irrelevant for ordinary believers," at the core of John Paul II vision is the belief "that St. John of the Cross's teachings concern the normal development of the supernatural life of faith and love" (Waldstein, TOB, p. 87).

2e. "Spiritual progress tends toward ever more intimate union with Christ. This union is called 'mystical' because it participates in the mystery of Christ … and, in him, in the mystery of the Holy Trinity. God calls us all to this intimate union with him, even if the special graces or extraordinary signs of this mystical life are granted only to some for the sake of manifesting the gratuitous gift given to all" (CCC 2014).

POINTS TO PONDER

Does the call to be a "mystic" seem beyond reach? Does it seem "not for me"? If so, why? Do you think if God wants you to be an "every-day mystic" that he will not also provide the means?

The mystics speak of three stages along the way of the interior life: the *purgative way*, the *illuminative way*, and the *unitive way*.

> **3a.** "In reality, these are not three distinct ways, but three aspects of the same way, along which Christ calls everyone" (MI, p. 28).

The Purgative Stage

This first stage involves the firm resolve to follow God's commandments, despite the rebellion of our fallen nature. It demands a firm commitment of the will to what is good and a willingness to be "purged" of disordered desires and attractions.

- In this stage we learn how to restrain ourselves from sin. With the help of God's grace, we are strengthened in our will to act *against* the disorder of our passions.

- In the language of St. Thomas Aquinas, such a person is "continent," but not yet *virtuous*.

> **3b.** Continence falls short of being virtue since virtue presupposes a right desire, and this is lacking in the continent man (see St. Thomas, *Summa*, Prima Secundae, q. 58, a. 3, ad 2).

> **3c.** "*Human virtues* … order our passions … They make possible ease, self-mastery, and joy in leading a morally good life" (CCC 1804).

> **3d.** "Observance of the commandments, properly understood, is synonymous with the purgative way: it means conquering sin, moral evil in its various guises. And this leads to gradual inner purification. It also enables us to discover values. And hence we conclude that the purgative way leads organically into the illuminative way" (MI, p. 28).

The Illuminative Stage

In the illuminative stage, God's light "illuminates" our lives so that we come to see ever more clearly reality as God created it to be. We come inwardly to value that which God values and desire that which God desires.

- At this stage we move from mere "continence" to *virtue*. We see that which is true, good, and beautiful and desire it with all our hearts.

- At this stage we are experiencing more and more "the freedom for which Christ has set us free" (Gal 5:1).

3e. "Values are lights which illuminate existence and, as we work on our lives, they shine ever more brightly on the horizon. So side by side with observance of the commandments – which has an essentially purgative meaning – we develop virtues. For example, in observing … the commandment: 'You shall not commit adultery!' we acquire the virtue of purity, and this means that we come to an ever greater awareness of the gratuitous beauty of the human body, of masculinity and femininity. This gratuitous beauty becomes a light for our actions" (MI, pp. 28-29).

3f. "With the passage of time, if we persevere in following Christ our Teacher, we feel less and less burdened by the struggle against sin, and we enjoy more and more the divine light which pervades all creation. This is most important, because it allows us to escape from a situation of constant inner exposure to the risk of sin – even though, on this earth, the risk always remains present to some degree – so as to move with ever greater freedom within the whole created world. This same freedom and simplicity characterizes our relations with other human beings, including those of the opposite sex" (MI, p. 29).

The Unitive Stage

If the purgative and illuminative stages represent a kind of "betrothal" of our lives to God – the beginning and maturing of a divine love affair – this final stage represents the consummation of the marriage, the fullest expression of union with God possible in this life.

3g. "This spiritual marriage is incomparably greater than the spiritual betrothal, for it is a total transformation in the Beloved, in which each surrenders the entire possession of self to the other with a certain consummation of the union of love … Just as in the consummation of carnal marriage there are two in one flesh … so also when the spiritual marriage between God and the soul is consummated, there are two natures in one spirit and love" (St. John of the Cross, Commentary on stanza 22:3 of the *Spiritual Canticle*, see TOB, p. 31).

3h. To the degree that we enter this unitive way we "can find God in everything … Created things cease to be a danger for us as once they were, particularly while we were still at the purgative stage of our journey. Creation, and other people in particular, not only regain their true light, given to them by God the Creator, but, so to speak, they lead us to God himself, in the way that he willed to reveal himself to us: as Father, Redeemer, and Spouse" (MI, p. 30).

"I THINK IT POSSIBLE TO AFFIRM THAT THE MORE NECESSARY THE TRUTH THE LESS IT IS PRACTICED BY SPIRITUAL PERSONS."

– ST. JOHN OF THE CROSS

"THE MAN WHO PRAYS … TRIES TO APPROACH THE LORD AND THUS SEEKS TO ENTER INTO NUPTIAL UNION WITH HIM."

– CARDINAL RATZINGER/BENEDICT XVI

Summary

- John Paul II's TOB is deeply rooted in the mystical theology of Saint John of the Cross. According to him, the spousal analogy illuminates the whole breadth of Christian teaching and experience. Christians are called to mystical marriage with God.

- To be a "mystic" means to live all of life from "within" the *great mystery* of Christ's spousal union with the Church – to be taken up by it, to be aflame with divine love. Each of us is called to be an "every day mystic."

- There are three stages along the way of the interior life: the *purgative way*, in which we learn to obey God's law and are gradually purged of our sinful inclinations; the *illuminative way*, in which we come to see more and more the divine light that pervades all of creation; and the *unitive way*, in which we experience a deep, transforming union with God.

STUDY QUESTIONS FOR:

SESSION 2: "NUPTIAL UNION": A CALL TO DEEP INTIMACY WITH GOD

1. Before studying John Paul II's TOB, had you ever thought of marriage and spousal union as an analogy for understanding the whole Christian life?

2. In what ways is it appropriate to apply the surrender of spouses in sexual union to the surrender of our hearts and lives to God? Where does the analogy lie? Where does the analogy fall short?

3. Have you ever heard about the "three ways" of the interior life? Where might you be in your own journey? What practical steps can I take to continue on my journey?

4. In your own words, explain the difference between continence and virtue.

5. It seems that many teachers of the faith imply that the purgative stage of the journey is all we can realistically expect in this life; as if a life of "virtue" meant no more than learning how to restrain ourselves from sin by force of will. John Paul II shows us that, if we persevere in following Christ, we can and should expect more, much more! In fact, settling for less can actually be a form of sinfulness. Why might that be so?

6. Explain the difference between looking lustfully at the human body and coming to see "the gratuitous beauty of the human body" as John Paul II describes it.

CHRIST
APPEALS TO THE
Beginning

Session 3
THE BODY: A WITNESS TO LOVE

1. REVIEW OF PREVIOUS SERIES

Key points from Session Three: *"Man and Woman He Created Them"*

- By pointing us back to "the beginning," Christ not only re-establishes God's original plan for man and woman as the norm, he also provides the *power* for us to live it.

- *Original solitude* refers not only to the man being without the woman (see Gen 2:18), but also to the fact that the human being (male and female) is alone in the visible world as a *person*. Persons have self-knowledge, self-possession, and freedom as the capacity to love God and one another.

- *Original unity* refers to the call of man and woman to live in a relationship that mirrors the inner life of the Trinity. We image God not only as individuals, but also through the holy communion of man and woman and the blessing of fertility.

- *Original nakedness* reveals the "spousal meaning of the body" which is the body's capacity of expressing divine love. Nakedness without shame demonstrates that man and woman experienced sexual desire as nothing but the desire to love as God loves – through the sincere gift of self.

2. THE FIRST "KEY WORD" OF CHRIST

"Have you not read that he who made them from the beginning made them male and female and said, 'For this reason a man shall leave his father and mother and be joined to his wife, and the two shall become one flesh'? So they are no longer two but one ... 'For your hardness of heart Moses allowed you to divorce your wives, but from the beginning it was not so'" (Mt 19:4-8).

Unity of Spirituality and Sexuality

- Becoming *one flesh* refers "without doubt" to the conjugal act (see TOB, 10:2). But we must never be content to stop at the surface of human sexuality, at merely the physical reality.

- Human sexuality always takes us to the deepest *spiritual* reality of the human being. It is there that we find the deepest truth about our creation as male and female.

2a. Human sexuality "is by no means something purely biological, but concerns the innermost being of the human person" (FC 11).

2b. "The main reason it is difficult for people in the modern age, and particularly for modern intellectuals, to understand the Catholic vision of sex, [John Paul II] argues, is – biology." Reducing the body to something merely biological "prevents us from understanding and living sex in its full meaning. The nature of sex has become invisible through our Cartesian glasses" (Waldstein, TOB, p. 97).

2c. Rene Descartes "who formulated the principle … 'I think, therefore I am,' also gave the modern concept of man its distinctive dualistic character. It is typical of rationalism to make a radical contrast in man between spirit and body, between body and spirit. But man is a person in the unity of his body and his spirit. The body can never be reduced to mere matter: it is a *spiritualized body*, just as man's spirit is so closely united to the body that he can be described as *an embodied spirit*" (LF 19).

2d. "It is not sexuality which creates in a man and a woman the need to give themselves to each other, but, on the contrary, it is the need to give oneself, latent in every human person, which finds its outlet … in physical and sexual union, in matrimony. But the need … to give oneself to and unite with another person is deeper and connected with the spiritual existence of the person. It is not finally and completely satisfied simply by union with another human being. Considered in the perspective of the person's eternal existence, marriage is only a tentative solution of the problem of a union of persons through love" (LR, pp. 253-254).

The Original Power of the Marital Embrace

John Paul demonstrates how tragically superficial we have become in our understanding of sexual relations. Properly understood and lived, sexual union re-presents the *very power* at the origin of the universe.

2e. Genesis 2:24 shows "that every conjugal union … renews in some way the mystery of creation in all its original depth and vital power" (TOB 10:4). "When they unite with each other (in the conjugal act) so closely so as to become 'one flesh,' man and woman rediscover every time and in a special way the mystery of creation" (TOB 10:2).

The "Virginal Value" of the Marital Embrace

We also tend to have a very superficial understanding of "virginity." John Paul expands our understanding of "virginity" to include in some way the purity of marital love and union.

- In the language of John Paul II, it seems the "virginal value" of man refers to the original integrity of body and soul that both man and woman experienced before sin.

"SHOULD HE ASPIRE TO BE PURE SPIRIT AND TO REJECT THE FLESH AS PERTAINING TO HIS ANIMAL NATURE ALONE, THEN SPIRIT AND BODY WOULD BOTH LOSE THEIR DIGNITY. ON THE OTHER HAND, SHOULD HE DENY THE SPIRIT AND CONSIDER MATTER, THE BODY, AS THE ONLY REALITY, HE WOULD LIKEWISE LOSE HIS GREATNESS."

– POPE BENEDICT XVI

"AUTHENTIC MARRIED LOVE IS CAUGHT UP INTO DIVINE LOVE."

– *CATECHISM OF THE CATHOLIC CHURCH* (1639)

- Man loses his "virginity" in this sense at the very moment of the original sin when he experiences a rupture in his body-soul integrity.

- Lustful sexual union, like pouring salt on a wound, always exacerbates this rift. Sexual union flowing from the power of the sacrament of marriage, however, heals this rift and, in this way, allows spouses gradually to reclaim the original "virginal value" of their humanity.

> **2f.** When, through the grace of redemption, man and woman become one-flesh, they are "returning to the union in humanity ('flesh from my flesh and bone from my bones') that allows them to recognize each other … and to call each other by name, as they did the first time. This means reliving in some way man's original virginal value" (TOB 10:2).

3. MAN IN THE DIMENSION OF THE GIFT

"Gift" is an essential category for understanding the human being properly – that is, for establishing an "adequate anthropology" (see TOB 13:2).

- "Gift" refers in the first place to God's self-giving in creation. In God's description of the goodness of creation ("Behold, it is very good"), we see that "God has no other reason for creating than his love and goodness" (CCC 293).

- God creates man to share in his own life (which is itself "eternal giving"). This is the utterly gratuitous "gift" of creation.

Re-presenting the Divine Gift

God initiates his self-gift by creating us in his image and for "our own sakes." "It follows, then, that man can only find himself through the sincere gift of self" (GS 24).

- In the original covenant, man (male and female) receives this gift and gives himself back to God.

- Man and woman image and re-present (or, as theologians say "recapitulate") the gift of God in creation by becoming a gift to each other.

> **3a.** "The dimension of gift is decisive for the essential truth and depth of the meaning of original solitude-unity-nakedness" (TOB 13:2).

> **3b.** "This is *the body: a witness* to creation as a fundamental gift, and therefore a witness *to Love as the source from which this same giving springs.* Masculinity-femininity – namely, sex – is the original sign of [God's] creative donation … This is the meaning with which sex enters into the theology of the body" (TOB 14:4).

"ALL MARRIED LIFE IS A GIFT; BUT THIS BECOMES MOST EVIDENT WHEN THE SPOUSES, IN GIVING THEMSELVES TO EACH OTHER IN LOVE, BRING ABOUT THAT ENCOUNTER WHICH MAKES THEM 'ONE FLESH.'"

– POPE JOHN PAUL II

3c. "Man appears in the visible world as the highest expression of the divine gift, because he bears within himself the inner dimension of the gift" (TOB 19:3).

3d. The "concept of 'giving' cannot refer to nothing. It indicates the one who gives, and the one who receives the gift, as well as the relation established between them" (TOB 13:4).

3e. The "giving and accepting [of] the gift interpenetrate in such a way that the very act of giving becomes acceptance, and acceptance transforms itself into giving" (TOB 17:4).

Summary

- Human sexuality always takes us to the deepest *spiritual* reality of the human being. It is there that we find the deepest truth about our creation as male and female. Reducing the body to something merely biological prevents us from seeing sex in its full meaning.

- Sexual union in God's plan is a participation in the very power of creation and redemption. When this union flows from the power of the sacrament of marriage, it helps to heal the rift in us caused by sin and, in this way, allows spouses gradually to reclaim their original "virginal value."

- "Gift" is an essential category for understanding the human being properly. It refers in the first place to God's self-giving in creation. God creates man to share in his own life (which is itself "eternal giving"). "It follows, then, that man can only find himself through the sincere gift of self" (GS 24).

- The body is *a witness* to creation as a fundamental gift, and therefore a witness *to God's Love* which is at the source of creation. This is the meaning with which sex – our creation as male and female – enters into the theology of the body.

STUDY QUESTIONS FOR:

SESSION 3: THE BODY: A WITNESS TO LOVE

1. Why do you think sexuality and spirituality are often considered divergent and conflicting realms?

2. People often think sex is somehow "better" when God is kept out of the picture ("*Keep God out of the bedroom*!"). Where does this sentiment come from?

3. Why did God create us male and female? Why are there two sexes? (It's true that part of the reason is to continue the species, but this "naturalistic" explanation is terribly reductive. Think big!).

4. What did the word "virginity" mean to you growing up. What does it mean to you now? What connotations (good and/or bad) does that word have for you?

5. Have you ever heard that a truly loving marital embrace is meant to help restore a person's "virginity" (or "virginal value" as John Paul II put it)? What thoughts, emotions, or questions does this idea raise in you?

6. What do you think it means to "find yourself through the sincere gift of self"? What are some examples of "sincere self-giving." How is the sexual union itself meant to be an expression of this?

7. John Paul II says that the body is a "witness to God's Love." Is this how the modern world understands the body? Is this how you see your own body? If not why not?

Session 4
THE BODY: SIGN OF GOD'S MYSTERY

1. THE SPOUSAL MEANING OF THE BODY

Giving and Receiving the Gift

The "spousal meaning of the body" is the defining term of the entire teaching. The call to be a "gift" is stamped right in our bodies in the mystery of sexual difference.

- A man's body does not make sense by itself. Nor does a woman's. Seen in light of each other we discover the unmistakable plan of the Creator.

- In the spousal meaning of the body we discover that God's image ("love" and "gift") is "impressed in the body from the beginning" (TOB 13:2).

  1a. The "spousal meaning of the body … constitutes the fundamental component of human existence in the world" (TOB 15:5). Therefore, "the spousal meaning of the body … is important and indispensable for knowing who man is and who he ought to be" (TOB 18:4).

  1b. The spousal meaning of the body refers to the body's *"power to express love: precisely that love in which the human person becomes a gift* and – through this gift – fulfills the very meaning of his being and existence" (TOB 15:1).

  1c. The spousal meaning of the body also indicates the "power and deep availability for the 'affirmation of the person' [as] someone unique and unrepeatable, someone chosen by eternal Love. The 'affirmation of the person' is nothing other than welcoming the gift" (TOB 15:4).

  1d. "Christ's words, which flow from the divine depth of the mystery of redemption, allow us to discover and strengthen the bond that exists between the dignity of the human being (of the man or the woman) and the spousal meaning of his body. On the basis of this meaning, they allow us to understand and bring about the mature freedom of the gift, which expresses itself in one way in indissoluble marriage and in another by abstaining from marriage for the kingdom of God. In these different ways, Christ 'fully reveals man to man himself and makes his supreme vocation clear' [GS, 22]" (TOB 86:8).

Freedom of the Gift

The first man and woman did not experience sexual desire as a compulsive urge imposing itself on them. Sexual desire arose in the deep recesses of personal freedom and was experienced as a yearning to make a sincere gift of oneself to the other *and* to receive the other's sincere gift.

- The freedom of the gift is the freedom to *bless*, which is freedom from the desire to *grasp* and *possess*. To grasp or possess the other would be to "extort the gift."

- This was an experience permeated by grace. Lust, as a result of original sin, will attack this freedom at its roots.

  1e. Man and woman are both naked without shame "because they are *free with the very freedom of the gift*. This freedom lies exactly at the basis of the spousal meaning of the body" (TOB 15:1).

  1f. "Here we mean freedom above all as *self-mastery* (self-dominion)." Such freedom "is indispensable *in order for man to be able to* ... 'find himself fully' through a 'sincere gift of self' [GS, 24]" (TOB 15:2).

2. Mystery of Original Innocence

Gift to the Human Heart

We know man and woman were "innocent" precisely because they were naked without shame (see Gen 2:25). This innocence "is holiness itself" (TOB 19:5).

- The mystery of original innocence/holiness was a human participation in *divine grace*. "Grace" and "gift" are almost synonymous here.

- Grace is God's holiness and power and love penetrating the creature.

  2a. "If creation is a gift given to man ... then *its fullness* and deepest dimension is *determined by grace*." And grace is none other than man's "participation in the inner life of God himself, in his holiness" (TOB 16:3).

  2b. Grace is "that mysterious *gift made to man's innermost [being] – to the human heart – that allows* both the man and the woman *to exist* from the "beginning" *in the reciprocal relationship of the disinterested gift of self*" (TOB 16:3).

  2c. Holiness "is measured according to the 'great mystery' in which the Bride responds with the gift of love to the gift of the Bridegroom" (MD 27).

> "IN REGAINING SELF-MASTERY IT MAY WELL BE NECESSARY AT FIRST TO 'CAGE' CONCUPISCENCE DESIRE BY FORCE OF WILL. BUT *THIS IS ONLY A FIRST STEP* ... THE ULTIMATE ROLE OF THE WILL IS NOT TO TYRANNIZE OR REPRESS THE PASSIONS, BUT TO DIRECT THEM WITH THE TRANSFORMING POWER OF GRACE TOWARD THE TRUTH OF SELF-GIVING LOVE."
>
> – FROM *THEOLOGY OF THE BODY EXPLAINED*

2d. "According to the words of Sacred Scripture, God penetrates the creature, who is completely 'naked' before him" (TOB 12:5, n. 22).

Original Happiness

"Original happiness" refers to the original beatifying (supremely happy, blissful) experience of man and woman's communion with God and with each other in the state of innocence. This foreshadows (even if only dimly) the beatifying communion of heaven.

> **2e.** *"The revelation and discovery of the spousal meaning of the body explain man's original happiness"* (TOB 15:5).

> **2f.** "Happiness is being rooted in Love. Original happiness speaks to us about the 'beginning' of man, who emerged from love and initiated love … One can define this 'beginning' also as the original and beatifying immunity from shame as the result of love" (TOB 16:2).

Marriage as the "Primordial Sacrament"

Since the "one flesh" reality of marriage refers right from the beginning to the "great mystery" of Christ's union with the Church, John Paul describes marriage as the *primordial sacrament*.

- All of creation is "sacramental" in that it reveals something of the mystery of its Creator. But this "sacramentality of the world" reaches its fulfillment (or crown) in man created in the image of God as male and female.

- Man, in turn, reaches his fulfillment through the sincere gift of self which was realized in an original way through the union in "one flesh."

> **2g.** In the original awareness of the spousal meaning of the body "a primordial *sacrament* is constituted, understood as a *sign that* efficaciously *transmits in the visible world the invisible mystery hidden in God from eternity*. And this is the mystery of Truth and Love, the mystery of divine life, in which man really participates" (TOB 19:4).

> **2h.** "The sacrament, as a visible sign, is constituted with man, inasmuch as he is a 'body,' through his 'visible' masculinity and femininity. The body, in fact, and only the body, is capable of making visible what is invisible: the spiritual and the divine. It has been created to transfer into the visible reality of the world the mystery hidden from eternity in God, and thus to be a sign of it" (TOB 19:4).

> **2i.** God "impressed his own form on the flesh ..in such a way that even what was visible might bear the divine form" (CCC 704).

> **2j.** "Against this vast background we fully understand the words in Genesis 2:24 that are constitutive of the sacrament of Marriage: 'For this reason a man will leave his father and his mother and unite with his wife, and the two will be one flesh'" (TOB 19:5).

> "THERE IS NO ESCAPE FROM THE BURNING DESIRE WITHIN US FOR THE TRUE, THE GOOD , THE BEAUTIFUL. EACH OF US LIVES WITH THE UNEXTINGUISHABLE EXPECTATION THAT LIFE IS SUPPOSED TO MAKE SENSE AND SATISFY US DEEPLY. EVEN THE MOST JADED ATHEIST FEELS CHEATED IF HE DOESN'T EXPERIENCE MEANING, PURPOSE PEACE – IN A WORD – HAPPINESS IN THIS LIFE. BUT JUST WHERE DOES THIS UNIVERSAL EXPECTATION FOR PERSONAL FULFILLMENT COME FROM? IT ISN'T SOMETHING WE DRUM UP OR MANUFACTURE ON OUR OWN. RATHER, THE BURNING YEARNING FOR 'WHAT IS REAL' IS INCORPORATED INTO OUR DIVINE DESIGN. THIS BURNING CAN LEAD EITHER TO THE TORMENT OF PAIN OR THE TORRENT OF LOVE. IT WILL EITHER CONSUME US OR CONSUMMATE US."
>
> – PETER JOHN CAMERON, O. P.

3. "Knowledge" and Procreation

"Adam knew his wife Eve, *and she conceived*" (Gen 4:1).

- These words are like a "seal" guaranteeing that God's original plan for man and woman continues throughout history despite the tragedy of sin (see TOB 22:5).

- The goodness of human life and of the sexual relationship continues to assert itself in the face of all that attacks it. All hope in a savior is placed here …

    3a. "When it speaks of 'knowledge' here … the Bible indicates the deepest essence of the reality of shared married life" (TOB 20:4).

    3b. "Sin and death have entered into man's history *in some way through the very heart of that unity that had from the 'beginning' been formed by man and woman,* created and called to become 'one flesh' (Gen 2:24)" (TOB, 20:1).

    3c. In the mystery of this biblical *knowledge* "life struggles always anew with the inexorable prospect of death, and always overcomes it … And both man and woman affirm [the victory of life] in the new man whom they generate … Despite all the experiences of his own life, despite the sufferings, the disappointments in himself, his sinfulness, and, finally, despite the inevitable prospect of death, man always continues, however, to place 'knowledge' at the 'beginning' of 'generation'; in this way he seems to participate in that first 'vision' of God himself [who] 'saw everything … and indeed, it was good.' And always anew [with every act of 'knowledge'] he confirms the truth of these words" (TOB 22:7).

Points to Ponder

If the conception of a child is a sign that life conquers death, what might a couple be saying with their bodies when they render their sexual union sterile?

Summary

- The "spousal meaning of the body" is the fundamental element of human existence in the world. It is the *power* of the body to image and express divine love. By living the true spousal meaning of our bodies – that is, by becoming a *free* gift to others – we fulfill the very meaning of our being and existence.

- *Original happiness* refers to the original beatifying (supremely happy, blissful) experience of man and woman's communion with God and with each other in the state of *original innocence*. This foreshadows (even if only dimly) the beatifying communion of heaven.

- Since the "one flesh" reality of marriage refers right from the beginning to the "great mystery" of Christ's union with the Church, John Paul describes marriage as the *primordial sacrament*. Only the body is capable of making the eternal mystery of God visible.

- "Adam knew his wife Eve, *and she conceived*" (Gen 4:1). These words are like a "seal" guaranteeing that God's original plan for man and woman continues throughout history despite the tragedy of sin. Every child conceived under the heart of a woman is a sign that love and life conquers sin and death.

STUDY QUESTIONS FOR:

SESSION 4: THE BODY: SIGN OF GOD'S MYSTERY

1. What makes the *spousal meaning of the body* the "fundamental component of human existence in the world"? Why is it indispensable for knowing who we are and who we are supposed to be?

2. Do animals have a spousal meaning attributed to their bodies? Why or why not?

3. Is the spousal meaning of the body to be equated with sexual intercourse? Is marriage the only way to live the spousal meaning of the body? If not, how else can we live it?

4. Why does the human being long for happiness? Where does that longing come from?

5. What are the ways I seek to satisfy the longing for happiness in myself? Is it possible to be as happy as man and woman were before sin?

6. What does it mean to call marriage the "primordial sacrament"?

7. How does the body reveal the mystery that has been hidden in God for all eternity?

8. Why is the conception of a child a sign of redemption? What does it imply to reject the possibility of conception in the midst of engaging in that act that is intended by God to lead to conception?

CHRIST
APPEALS TO THE
Human Heart

Session 5

THE HEART: A BATTLEFIELD BETWEEN LOVE AND LUST

1. REVIEW OF PREVIOUS SERIES

Key points from Session Four: *"Man and Woman He Redeemed Them"*

- Lust is the inversion of sexual desire which resulted when the first man and woman closed their hearts to divine love. Shame, as a response to lust, is a natural form of self defense against the danger of being treated as an object for sexual use.

- Christ calls us to rediscover a *pure* way of looking at others capable of respecting the "gratuitous beauty" of the human body in its masculinity and femininity.

- Christ did not die on a cross and rise from the dead to give us more "rules" to follow. He came to change our hearts so that we would no longer need the rules. To the degree that God's law (*ethic*) is written on our hearts (*ethos*), we are *free from the law* – not free to break it, but free to fulfill it.

- The redemption of the body is the foundation of everything John Paul II teaches in his TOB. It refers not only to the hope of resurrection at the end of time, but is a power at work in us *now* able to do far more than we think or imagine. It is able to transform our experience of the body and sexuality.

2. THE SECOND "KEY WORD" OF CHRIST

Adultery in the "Heart"

"You have heard that it was said, 'You shall not commit adultery.' But I say to you that everyone who looks at a woman lustfully has already committed adultery with her in his heart" (Mt 5:27-28).

- Christ's words are not so much a condemnation of the human heart, but a calling.

- They call us to another way of seeing the body, another way of understanding and living the gift of human sexuality.

  2a. Whoever allows these words to act in him will "hear in his innermost [being] the echo, as it were, of that 'beginning,' of that good 'beginning' to which Christ appealed on another occasion" (TOB 46:5).

POINTS TO PONDER

The media and even mental health professionals have fostered the notion that sexual restraint is inherently bad for us – and many of us have believed them. But does this make sense? We encourage self-restraint all the time: don't hit your sister, share your toys, don't eat the whole cheese cake, don't pass gas in public. These, and a great multitude of other restraints, are considered normal and healthy. But why do people cry "pathology" as soon as someone suggests restraint for the sexual appetite?

2b. Christ's words "demand, so to speak, that man enters into his full image" (TOB 25:2). Man *"must rediscover the lost fullness of his humanity and want to regain it"* (TOB 43:7).

Christian Ethos: A Living Morality

"Unless your righteousness exceeds that of the scribes and the Pharisees, you will never enter the kingdom of heaven" (Mt 5:20). "You blind Pharisee! First cleanse the inside of the cup and of the plate, that the outside also may be clean" (Mt 23:26).

- We all know it is possible to be fixated on merely following rules. But such "legalism" or "moralism" does not, in itself, lead to holiness.

- As Pope Benedict XVI insists: "Being Christian is not the result of an ethical choice." It's the result of "the encounter with ... a person, which gives life a new horizon and a decisive direction" (DC 1).

    2c. Ethos refers to "the inner form, the soul, as it were, of human morality ... To reach it, it is not enough to stop 'on the surface' of human actions, but one must penetrate precisely the interior" (TOB, 24:3).

    2d. The ethos of redemption is a "living morality ... in which the very meaning of being human is realized" (TOB 24:3).

    2e. "It is impossible to keep the Lord's commandment by imitating the divine model from outside; there has to be a vital participation, coming from the depths of the heart" (CCC 2842).

    2f. "Christian ethos is characterized by *a transformation of the human person's conscience and attitudes ... such as to express and realize the value of the body and sex* according to the Creator's original plan" (TOB 45:3).

3. THE MAN OF CONCUPISCENCE

A Three-Fold Lust

"For all that is in the world, the lust of the flesh and the lust of the eyes and the pride of life, is not of the Father, but is of the world. And the world passes away, and the lust of it; but he who does the will of God abides forever" (1 Jn 2:16-17).

- The "world" St. John refers to here is not the "very good" world God created for man, but what results when man breaks the covenant with God.

- "Concupiscence" refers to the disordering of our passions that resulted from original sin. As St. John indicates, concupiscence is broader than the disorder of the sexual appetite, but often refers to this.

- Concupiscence comes from sin, inclines to sin, but is not itself a sin. It "cannot harm those who do not consent" to it (see CCC 1264).

- Only when a person has engaged his will to follow the promptings of concupiscence has he sinned. Simply recognizing those promptings within one's heart is not a sin.

> **3a.** "Concupiscence is to be explained as a lack, as a lack, however, that plunges its roots into the original depth of the human spirit" (TOB 27:2).

> **3b.** It "is as if the 'man of concupiscence' … had simply ceased … to remain above the world of [animals]. It is as if he experienced a specific *fracture of the personal integrity of his own body, particularly in that which determines its sexuality*" (TOB 28:4).

Fallen Man is Depraved (But Not Utterly Depraved)

Original sin caused "a deprivation of original holiness and justice, but human nature *has not been totally corrupted*: it is wounded … and inclined to sin" but not utterly depraved (CCC 405 emphasis added).

> **3c.** "The first Protestant reformers … taught that original sin has *radically perverted* man and *destroyed his freedom*." In this view, "the tendency to sin (concupiscentia) … would be insurmountable" (CCC 406 emphasis added).

> **3d.** "The human body in its masculinity and femininity has almost lost the power of expressing this love in which the human person becomes a gift." We add the adverb "almost" because the "spousal meaning of the body has not become totally foreign to that heart: *it has not been totally suffocated in it by concupiscence, but only habitually threatened.* The 'heart' has become a battlefield between love and concupiscence. The more concupiscence dominates the heart, the less the heart experiences the spousal meaning of the body" (TOB 32:3).

> **3e.** [paraphrasing] We must learn with perseverance and consistency the meaning of our bodies, the meaning of our sexuality. We must learn this not only in the abstract (although this, too, is necessary), but above all in the interior reactions of our own "hearts." This is a "science" which cannot really be learned only from books, because it is a question here of deep knowledge of our interior life. Deep in the heart we learn to distinguish between what, on the one hand, composes the great riches of sexuality and sexual attraction, and what, on the other hand, bears only the sign of lust. And although these internal movements of the heart can sometimes be confused with each other, we have been *called by Christ to acquire a mature and complete evaluation allowing us to distinguish and judge the various movements of our hearts.* "And it should be added that this task *can* be carried out and that it is truly worthy of man" (TOB 48:4).

Summary

- It is not enough to follow God's commandments in an exterior way. Christ's words about lust in the heart call us to a new ethos, a new way of life. We must come to realize the lost fullness of our true humanity and long to regain it.

- "Concupiscence" refers to the disordering of our passions that resulted from original sin. Concupiscence comes from sin, inclines us to sin, but is not itself a sin. Concupiscence is the cause of a great battle in our hearts between love and lust.

- We have almost lost the power of expressing that love in which the human person becomes a gift through his body. We must relearn the true meaning of our sexuality not only in the abstract, but above all in the depths of our own "hearts." With God's help, this task *can* be carried out and it is truly worthy of man.

STUDY QUESTIONS FOR:

SESSION 5: THE HEART: A BATTLEFIELD BETWEEN LOVE AND LUST

1. What is the relationship between the "new ethos" of redemption and the purgative, illuminative, and unitive stages of the interior life?

2. How can we regain the lost fullness of our humanity? What does this entail day to day?

3. How was Christian morality presented to you growing up? Did you consider Christianity to be a list of rules to follow?

4. What are the dangers of reducing Christianity to a legalistic following of rules? Why do you think Christianity is often perceived as such?

5. Everyone can recognize the "pull" of concupiscence within himself. What does Christ call us to do about it in the Sermon on the Mount?

6. What are the hidden dangers of conceiving of the human being as "utterly depraved"?

7. What practical steps can I take to learn that "science" (as John Paul II calls it) of discerning the inner movements and reactions of my heart?

Session 6

THE DIMENSIONS OF LUST IN THE HEART

1. THE ENTRANCE OF SHAME

Casting Doubt on the Gift

"You will not die. For God knows that when you eat of it your eyes will be opened, and you will be like God, knowing good and evil" (Gen 3:4-5).

- We're created for *infinity*, but as "finites" we can't access it. This places us in a radical posture of dependence on the "Infinite One" to grant us the *gift* of himself. Do we believe he will?

- Faith leads to "receptivity" before God. Lack of faith leads to "grasping."

- When man conceives of God as a tyrant, he is goaded to do battle against his Maker so as not to be enslaved. Do we believe, as John Paul insists, that the "paradigm of master-slave is foreign to the Gospel"? (CTH, p. 226)

- When we deny the gift in God, we lose our ready ability to be a gift to one another.

    1a. Woman "is the representative and the archetype of the whole human race: she *represents the humanity* which belongs to all human beings, both men and women" (MD 4).

    1b. "By casting doubt in his heart on the deepest meaning of the gift … man turns his back … on 'the Father.' He in some sense casts him from his heart" (TOB 26:4).

    1c. "*This is truly the key for interpreting reality … Original sin, then, attempts to abolish fatherhood*" (CTH, p. 228).

    1d. "Christ, *through the revelation of the mystery of the Father and his love*, fully reveals man to himself and makes his supreme calling clear" (GS 22; emphasis added).

    1e. If original sin is the denial of the gift, "*faith*, in its deepest essence, is *the openness* of the human heart to the gift: *to God's self-communication in the Holy Spirit*" (DV 51).

> WE MIGHT READ THE SERPENT'S TEMPTATION LIKE THIS: "GOD DOESN'T LOVE YOU. HE'S NOT LOOKIN' OUT FOR YOU. HE'S A TYRANT, A SLAVE-DRIVER WHO WANTS TO KEEP YOU FROM WHAT YOU REALLY WANT. THAT'S WHY HE TOLD YOU NOT TO EAT FROM THAT TREE. IF YOU WANT LIFE AND HAPPINESS, IF YOU WANT TO BE 'LIKE GOD,' THEN YOU HAVE TO REACH OUT AND GRASP IT FOR YOURSELF BECAUSE GOD SURE AIN'T GONNA GIVE IT TO YOU."
>
> – FROM *THEOLOGY OF THE BODY FOR BEGINNERS*

Man Alienated from Original Love

"Then the eyes of both were opened, and they knew that they were naked; and they sewed fig leaves together and made themselves aprons … 'I was afraid, because I was naked; and I hid myself'" (Gen 3:7, 10).

- Shame is "the boundary experience" between our origin and our history. Nakedness once revealed participation in holiness/grace, now it reveals their loss.

- The body and gender difference are now "blamed" for the rupture caused by sin, but this is a "cover up" – almost an "excuse" not to face the disorder of the heart.

> **1f.** Shame touches man and woman at their "deepest level and seems to shake the very foundations of their existence" (TOB 27:1). From this moment on, shame will cause "a fundamental disquiet in the whole of human existence" (TOB 28:3).

> **1g.** Shame "reveals a *specific difficulty in sensing the human essentiality of one's own body*" (TOB 28:2).

> **1h.** "Shame has a twofold meaning: it indicates the threat to the value [of the person] and at the same time preserves this value in an interior way" (TOB 28:6).

2. The Distortion of Lust

The Second Discovery of Sex

The "'second' discovery of sex … differs radically from the first" (TOB 29:4). Rather than finding themselves united in their masculinity and femininity, sexual difference now divides them and sets them against each other (see TOB 30:5). Their original ability to share themselves "has been shattered" (see TOB 29:2).

- Because of their disobedience, the love of God "ex-spired" from their hearts. We cannot give what we do not have.

- Lust seeks "the sensation of sexuality" apart from a true communion of persons (see TOB 29:3).

> **2a.** "Concupiscence as such is not able to promote [the] communion of persons … *The relationship of the gift changes into a relationship of appropriation*" (TOB 32:6).

> **2b.** Because of sin, man and woman's "mutual attraction, the Creator's own gift, changed into a relationship of domination and lust" (CCC 1607).

"THE EXPENSE OF SPIRIT IN A WASTE OF SHAME IS LUST IN ACTION; AND TILL ACTION, LUST IS PERJURED, MURDEROUS, BLOODY, FULL OF BLAME, SAVAGE, EXTREME, RUDE, CRUEL, NOT TO TRUST; ENJOY'D NO SOONER BUT DESPISED STRAIGHT; PAST REASON HUNTED; AND NO SOONER HAD, PAST REASON HATED, AS A SWALLOWED BAIT, ON PURPOSE LAID TO MAKE THE TAKER MAD: MAD IN PURSUIT, AND IN POSSESSION SO; HAD, HAVING, AND IN QUEST TO HAVE, EXTREME; A BLISS IN PROOF, AND PROVED, A VERY WOE; BEFORE, A JOY PROPOSED; BEHIND, A DREAM. ALL THIS THE WORLD WELL KNOWS; YET NONE KNOWS WELL TO SHUN THE HEAVEN THAT LEADS MEN TO THIS HELL."

– WILLIAM SHAKESPEARE

2c. Lust "is not always plain and obvious; sometimes it is concealed, so that it passes itself off as 'love' … Does this mean that we should distrust the human heart? No! It is only to say that we must remain in control of it" (TOB 32:3).

An Apparent Inequality

"To the woman [God] said, 'in pain you shall bring forth children, yet your desire shall be for your husband and he shall dominate you'" (Gen 3:16).

- The whole of human history has been marked by various forms of male domination. Woman's special genius is now seen as a burden or even a curse.

- Throughout history, all that is feminine will experience a particular prejudice or even hatred (misogyny).

   2d. Lust and shame touch "the innermost [being] of both the male and female personality, even though in a different way" (TOB 31:4).

   2e. If lust and domination prevail "in the man, the desires that the woman directs toward him … can assume – and do assume – an analogous character. And, perhaps, at times, they precede the man's 'desire,' or even aim to arouse it and give it impetus" (TOB 31:3).

   2f. The "*man* ought to have been 'from the beginning' *the guardian of the reciprocity of the gift and of its true balance* … Although maintaining the balance of the gift seems to be something entrusted to both, the man has a special responsibility, as if it depended more on him whether the balance is kept or violated or even – if it has already been violated – reestablished" (TOB 33:2).

3. CORRUPTION OF THE SPOUSAL MEANING OF THE BODY

"Measure of the Heart"

The call to love "as God loves" is inscribed in the spousal meaning of the body. To the degree that we "look lustfully" we blind ourselves to this mystery. In this way recognizing or failing to recognize the spousal meaning of the body becomes a "measure" of our hearts.

- Lust "extorts the gift" and becomes the "antithesis of the gift" (see TOB 17:3).

- Lust, therefore, involves a "limitation, violation, or complete deformation" of the *spousal meaning of the body* (see TOB 31:6).

3a. Looking lustfully "indicates an experience of the value of the body in which its spousal meaning ceases to be spousal precisely because of concupiscence. What also ceases is its procreative meaning" (TOB 39:5). As a result, the body "loses its character as a sign" (TOB 40:4).

3b. Lust "tramples on the ruins of the spousal meaning of the body and … aims directly … *to satisfy only the body's sexual urge*" (TOB 40:4).

Loss of the Freedom of the Gift

With the dawn of concupiscence, sexual desire now manifests itself as "a quasi self-generating force … operating according to its own dynamics" (TOB 32:2). But there is "real power" flowing from the death and resurrection of Christ to restore our freedom!

3c. "Concupiscence … *deprives man, one could say, of the dignity of the gift*" because it "brings with it the loss of the interior freedom of the gift" (TOB 32:4, 6).

3d. "The new dimension of ethos is always linked with … the liberation of the heart from 'concupiscence'" (TOB 43:6).

Summary

- As creatures, we are radically dependant on our Creator for life, for love, for happiness. Faith leads to "receptivity" before God. Lack of faith leads to "grasping." If original sin is the denial of the gift, *faith*, in its deepest essence, is *the openness* of the human heart to God's gift of life, love, and happiness.

- The "second" discovery of sex differs radically from the first. Because of lust, the original ability of man and woman to share themselves has been shattered. Shame is now their lot. Both are deeply affected by this "new" situation, but woman seems to experience the effects of it more painfully.

- Lust involves a limitation, violation, or complete deformation of the *spousal meaning of the body*. It tramples on the ruins of the spousal meaning of the body and aims directly to satisfy only the body's sexual urge.

- Because of the rupture within us caused by sin, sexual desire now seems to have a mind of its own. It manifests itself almost as a self-generating force over which, it seems, the person has little control. But there is "real power" flowing from the death and resurrection of Christ to restore our freedom!

STUDY QUESTIONS FOR:

SESSION 6: DIMENSIONS OF LUST IN THE HEART

1. As Christopher mentioned in the lecture, if God really and truly desires to grant me the deepest yearning of my heart for happiness, then all I need do to be happy is open to *receive the gift*. Do I live a life of "receptivity" or "grasping"?

2. How does it make you feel to realize your utter dependence on God for life, for love, for happiness? Angry? Vulnerable? Trusting? Scared?

3. Most men and women seem to think that lust and shame (and the resulting pain) are just "normal," just "the way it is." How does it make you feel to realize that "in the beginning it was not so"? Do you have hope that love – the love we really yearn for – is possible?

4. How do men and women experience lust and shame differently? Do you think it is fair to say that throughout history there has been a particular prejudice against women, a particular burden that she has had to carry because of lust and shame? Discuss.

5. In what ways does lust violate, limit, or completely deform the *spousal meaning of the body*?

6. St. Paul exclaims that it is for freedom that Christ has set us free (see Gal 5)! How does this apply to our experience of sexual desire? Does it apply here?

7. Describe in your own words what "sexual redemption" means. What needs to be redeemed? Can it be redeemed? If so, how? And what does this mean for me, personally?

Session 7
The Law and the Heart

1. Three Aspects of Christ's Statement

It Was Said, "Do Not Commit Adultery"

Passing over from the Old Law to the "new ethos" of the Gospel demands a radical paradigm shift of God's people. We "are justified by [God's] grace as a gift, through the redemption which is in Christ Jesus" (Rom 3:24), not by "following the rules."

- Whoever would seek to justify himself by following the law has no need for Jesus. He has cut himself off from Christ and fallen away from grace (see Gal 5:4).

- "The law was given that grace might be sought; and grace was given that the law might be fulfilled" (St. Augustine).

  1a. "Love and life according to the Gospel cannot be thought of first and foremost as a kind of precept, because what they demand is beyond man's abilities. They are possible only as a result of a gift of God who heals, restores, and transforms the human heart by his grace." Living the Gospel, then, is *a possibility opened to man exclusively by grace*, by the gift of God, by his love" (VS 23, 24).

  1b. "The judgment about the body and sex expressed [in the Old Testament] is ... *marked by an objectivism* motivated by the intention of setting this area of human life in order. It is not concerned directly with the order of the 'heart' but with the order of social life as a whole, at the base of which stands, as always, marriage and the family" (TOB 36:3).

"Whoever Looks with Lust"

The Gospel ethos reveals that we cannot reduce the illicit to the illegal. A rightly formed conscience takes one deeper than mere legality.

- In other words, just because it is "legal" to do something doesn't in itself tell us whether it is "right" to do that thing.

- It is "legal" for married people to have sexual relations. But one must journey *into the heart* in order to evaluate what is truly happening.

  1c. The Sermon on the Mount makes "the transfer or shift *of the meaning of adultery from the 'body' to the 'heart'*" (TOB 38:1). "*The look expresses what is in the heart*" (TOB 39:4).

"WE OFTEN BELIEVE THAT OUR ETERNAL DESTINY WILL BE DETERMINED BY A SCALE WEIGHING OUR GOOD WORKS AGAINST OUR SINS. IF THIS IS THE CASE, WE SIMPLY CAN'T AFFORD TO ADMIT THE DEPTH OF SIN IN OUR LIVES; THE IMPLICATIONS ARE TOO DEVASTATING. SO WE RATIONALIZE OUR SIN AND CONTINUE TO COMFORT OURSELVES BY RECALLING THAT WE'RE NOT NEARLY AS BAD AS 'THOSE REALLY NASTY SINNERS DOWN THE STREET.' BUT WHERE IS THE DEATH AND RESURRECTION OF JESUS IN THIS VIEW OF SALVATION?"

– FROM *THE LOVE THAT SATISFIES*

1d. Prescriptions of the Old Testament such as "'Turn away your eyes from a shapely woman' (Sir 9:8) … are in some way close to Christ's appeal to the 'heart' … though one cannot say that they show any tendency to transform ethos in a fundamental way … Such a transformation of ethos had to await the Sermon on the Mount" (TOB 38:5-6). Here we encounter *"the possibility and the necessity of transforming* what has been weighed down by the concupiscence of the flesh" (TOB 47:5).

1e. "There were … under the regime of the Old Covenant, people who possessed the … grace of the Holy Spirit … Conversely, there exist carnal men under the New Covenant, still distanced from the perfection of the New Law" (St. Thomas Aquinas, CCC 1964).

"Has Committed Adultery in the Heart"

Christ's transfer of adultery from "the body" to "the heart" is a call to fulfill the law. "Think not that I have come to abolish the law and the prophets. I have come not to abolish them, *but to fulfill them*" (Mt 5:17). If "you are led by the Spirit, you are not under the law" (Gal 5:18).

- In as much as a person is "led by the Spirit" he no longer needs an external norm constraining him from committing adultery. He *does not desire* to commit adultery.

- Such a person is free from the "burden" of the law because the law is "written on his heart." Lust – even if he is still capable of it – no longer holds sway in his heart.

- Freedom from the law and the fulfillment of it are well summarized in Augustine's famous statement: "Love God, and do whatever you want."

1f. The Law "does not of itself give the strength, the grace of the spirit, to fulfill it. Because of sin, which it cannot remove, it remains a law of bondage" (CCC 1963).

1g. Christ's words show "how deep down it is necessary to go, how the innermost recesses of the human heart must be thoroughly revealed, so that this heart might become a place in which the law is 'fulfilled'" (TOB 43:5).

1h. "Adultery 'in the heart' is not committed only because the man 'looks' in this way at a woman who is not his wife, but *precisely because he looks in this way at a woman. Even* if he were to look in this way at … his wife, he would commit the same adultery 'in the heart'" (TOB 43:2).

1i. "Should we *fear* the severity of [Christ's] words, or rather *have confidence* in their salvific content, in their power?" (TOB 43:7).

[handwritten notes: Conscience takes us deeper than any law! not watering down His — reclaim original designed value]

2. Is the Heart Accused or Called?

Manichaeism

If we are to understand the proper sense of Christ's words, we must contend with the "deep seated habits" which spring from Manichaeism in our way of thinking and evaluating things (see TOB 46:1).

- Manichaeism sees the source of evil in matter and therefore condemns all that is bodily in man, especially sex (see TOB 44:5).

- The Manichaean way of seeing man's body and sexuality is "foreign to the Gospel" (TOB 45:5).

    2a. "While for the Manichaean mentality, the body and sexuality constitute … an 'anti-value,' for Christianity, on the contrary, they always remain a 'value not sufficiently appreciated'" (TOB 45:3).

    2b. Christ demands detachment from the evil of lust, but this does not mean in any way that the object of this desire (in this case, a woman) is an evil. Such a notion would signify a certain acceptance of the Manichaean attitude. It would not constitute a real and deep victory over the evil of lust. On the contrary, there would be concealed in this attitude the great danger of justifying lust to the detriment of the woman (see TOB 45:4).

    2c. We can see that the Manichaean condemnation of sex "might – and may always be – a loophole to avoid the requirements set in the Gospel" (TOB 44:6).

"Masters of Suspicion"

Redemption does not remove the consequences of original sin during our historical existence. We still suffer, get ill, grow old, struggle with weaknesses and the pull of concupiscence, etc. (see CCC, 978, 1226, 1264, 1426). Yet, the reality of lust must not cause us to hold the human heart in continual suspicion.

- A "master of suspicion" is a person who does not know or does not fully believe in the transforming power of the Gospel. Lust holds sway in his own heart so he projects the same onto everyone else.

- We must be careful not to fall into the trap of "holding the form of religion" while "denying the power of it" (2 Tim 3:5).

    2d. "Man cannot stop at casting the 'heart' into a state of continual and irreversible suspicion due to the manifestations of the concupiscence of the flesh … Redemption is a truth, a reality, in the name of which man must feel himself called, and 'called with effectiveness'" (TOB 46:4).

Points to Ponder

We must carefully examine our language to see where a Manichaean attitude might lurk, that is, where we might subtly or not so subtly be assigning evil to the body. For example, what does one typically ask before entering a person's bedroom: "Are you *decent*?" From the (authentically) Catholic perspective, what is the only proper response to this question, even if you are entirely naked?

2e. "The meaning of life is the antithesis of the [interpretation] 'of suspicion.'" This interpretation "is very different, *it is radically different* from the one we discover *in Christ's words* in the Sermon on the Mount. These words bring to light ... another vision of man's possibilities" (TOB 46:6).

2f. What "are the 'concrete possibilities of man'? And of which man are we speaking? Of man *dominated* by lust or of man *redeemed by Christ*? This is what is at stake: the *reality* of Christ's redemption. *Christ has redeemed us!* This means He has given us the possibility of realizing the *entire truth* of our being; He has set our freedom free from the *domination* of concupiscence. And if redeemed man still sins, this is not due to an imperfection of Christ's redemptive act, but to man's will not to avail himself of the grace which flows from that act. God's command is of course proportioned to man's capabilities; but to the capabilities of the man to whom the Holy Spirit has been given" (VS 103).

2635

Open our flesh to "Ideal" can't possibly live that

Summary

- Whoever seeks to justify himself by "following the rules" has no need for Jesus. What the Gospel demands is beyond our abilities. It becomes possible only as a result of God's grace, which heals, restores, and transforms the human heart.

- In the Sermon on the Mount, Christ shifts the meaning of adultery from the "body" to the "heart." Admonitions of the Old Testament such as "Turn away your eyes from a shapely woman" (Sir 9:8) retain all their wisdom for those bound by lust. They do not, however, transform our hearts. Such a transformation had to await Christ.

- A man who objectifies his wife also commits adultery "in the heart." Christ's words show how deep down it is necessary for us to go, how the innermost recesses of our hearts must be thoroughly revealed, so that our hearts might become a place in which the law is fulfilled.

- We must contend with the "deep seated habits" which spring from Manichaeism in our way of thinking about the body and sex. If Manichaeism says "body-bad," Christianity says "body-so-good we have yet to fathom it." Blaming the body for sin amounts to a "convenient" loophole for avoiding the purity required by the Gospel.

- A "master of suspicion" is a person who does not know or does not fully believe in the power of the Gospel. Lust holds sway in his own heart, so he projects the same onto everyone else. We mustn't condemn the heart to lust. Redemption is a truth in the name of which we must feel *called with power* to a new way of seeing and thinking.

STUDY QUESTIONS FOR:
SESSION 7: THE LAW AND THE HEART

1. Did you grow up thinking that you had to justify *yourself* by being a "good little boy/girl"? If so, where and why do you think religious education got so off track in this regard?

2. Did you grow up considering Christianity a list of rules to follow? Did you ever hear or realize that Christ offers us *real power* to live and experience sexual desire as God created it to be, as the power to love in God's image?

3. What does it mean to "pass-over" from the Old Testament law to the New Testament law?

4. How can lust manifest itself even in marriage? What do you think leads people to think it is "okay" to indulge lust within marriage?

5. The way a husband might objectify his wife seems more obvious perhaps. In what ways might a woman objectify her husband?

6. What is the difference between the "interpretation of suspicion" and wise moral discernment?

7. What ways have I, perhaps, been guilty of the "interpretation of suspicion"?

BLESSED ARE THE PURE OF HEART

6/21/10
disordered desires

1. "THE FREEDOM FOR WHICH CHRIST HAS SET US FREE"

"For freedom Christ has set us free; stand fast therefore, and do not submit again to a yoke of slavery … For you were called to freedom, brethren; only do not use your freedom as an opportunity for the flesh, but through love be servants of one another" (Gal 5:1, 13).

- The freedom necessary for love also provides the opportunity to indulge "the flesh." ("Flesh" does not mean "body bad." Flesh in the language of Paul is actually the human heart cut off from God's grace.)

- We must not remove the free choice we have to choose between good and evil. For in the same stroke we eradicate the freedom that is necessary to love. If we must chain ourselves to avoid sin, we are not free, we are *in chains.*

- If we are not free in this sense, we have yet to pass over from the Old to the New law.

X • True freedom is not liberty to indulge our compulsions, but liberation from our compulsions to indulge.

> **1a.** The "liberation of the heart from 'concupiscence' … is the condition of all life together in the truth" (TOB 43:6).

> **1b.** "The one who *lives … 'according to the flesh' … ceases to be capable of this freedom* for which 'Christ has set us free'; he also ceases to be suitable *for the true gift* of self, which is … organically linked with the spousal meaning of the human body." Indulging one's lusts is the "antithesis" and the "negation" of freedom (TOB 53:3).

> **1c.** The very manner in which we conceive the relationship of the sexes must be, to the greatest extent possible, freed from a purely impulse-oriented view and shaped according to the freedom and dignity of the person (see PC, p. 330). In this impulse-oriented view there seems to be a tendency to limit the possibility of virtue and magnify the "necessity of sin" in the sexual sphere. When we understand the possibilities of human freedom, we perceive the possibility of virtue based on self-control and sublimation (see PC, p. 286).

> "MAN UNDERSTANDS HIS LIBERTY ACCORDING TO WHETHER HE IS FREE."
>
> – POPE JOHN PAUL II

2. PURITY OF HEART

"Blessed are the pure in heart, for they shall see God" (Mt 5:8). "To the pure all things are pure, but to the corrupt and unbelieving nothing is pure" (Ti 1:15).

- Christian purity is not prudishness or puritanism! It does not involve a rejection or repression of our passions, but rather a redemption and transformation of them.

- Authentic purity recognizes that those parts of the body that fallen men think are "less honorable" actually deserve "all the greater honor" (1 Cor 12:23).

> **2a.** "Purity is the glory of the human body before God. It is the glory of God in the human body, through which masculinity and femininity are manifested" (TOB 57:3).

> **2b.** "Even now [purity of heart] enables us to see *according to* God … it lets us perceive the human body – ours and our neighbor's – as a temple of the Holy Spirit, a manifestation of divine beauty" (CCC 2519).

> **2c.** Man must learn "to be the authentic master of his own innermost impulses, like a watchman who watches over a hidden spring, and finally able to draw from all these impulses what is fitting for 'purity of the heart' (TOB 48:3).

> **2d.** "The task of purity … is not only (and not so much) abstaining … [there is] another function of the virtue of purity … another dimension – one could say – that is more positive than negative" (TOB 54:3). The positive dimension of purity "opens the way toward an ever more perfect discovery of the dignity of the human body" (TOB 58:6).

> **2e.** "Purity is a requirement of love. It is the dimension of the inner truth of love in man's 'heart'" (TOB49:7).

> **2f.** Purity of heart affords "'the absorption of shame by love.' Shame is, as it were, swallowed up by love, dissolved in it, so that the man and the woman are no longer ashamed to be sharing their experience of sexual values. This process is enormously important to sexual morality." This "does not mean that [shame (in its positive sense)] is eliminated or destroyed. Quite the contrary, it is reinforced." Yet where there is genuine love, shame (in the negative sense) "as the natural way of avoiding the utilitarian attitude [towards the body] loses its *raison d'etre* and gives ground. But only to the extent that a person loved in this way – and this is most important – is equally ready to give herself or himself in love" (LR, pp. 181-183)

"AS SOON AS YOU ENTERED [THE BAPTISMAL FONT], THEN, YOU DIVESTED YOURSELF OF YOUR GARMENT; THIS GESTURE SYMBOLIZED THE DIVESTING YOURSELF OF THE OLD MAN IN YOU WITH ALL HIS PRACTICES. DISROBED, YOU WERE NAKED, SYMBOLIZING IN THIS CHRIST WHO WAS NAILED NAKED TO THE CROSS, AND BY HIS VERY NUDITY DEFEATED THE PRINCIPALITIES AND POWERS, DRAGGING THEM INTO HIS TRIUMPHAL CORTEGE … O MARVELOUS THING, YOU WERE NAKED BEFORE EVERYONE AND YET YOU DID NOT BLUSH FOR SHAME. TRULY YOU REPRESENTED IN THIS THE IMAGE OF THE FIRST MAN, ADAM, WHO IN PARADISE WAS NAKED BUT WAS NOT ASHAMED."

– ST. CYRIL OF JERUSALEM

3. PORTRAYING THE HUMAN BODY IN ART

Can the naked body be portrayed in art without offending its dignity? What is the difference between the nakedness in the Sistine Chapel and the nakedness in pornography?

- A person of "developed sensitivity" can overcome "the limit of shame" in order to behold the naked body with a holy gaze. But this happens "only with difficulty and inner resistence" (see TOB 61:3).

- If appropriate portrayals of the body can help us *overcome* the limits of shame, inappropriate portrayals of the body *overstep* the limits of shame (see TOB 61:4).

- Pornography and appropriate art are distinguished by the intention of the "artist." Is the intention to arouse lust or to help us ponder the true beauty of the human person?

- We can say that the problem with pornography is not that it reveals too much of the person, but that it reveals far too little. In fact, it's goal is to *obscure the person*, effectively concealing the person's true beauty and mystery.

> **3a.** The portrayal of the naked body in art raises a "very delicate problem" (TOB 61:1) since "that 'element of the gift' is, so to speak, suspended in the dimension of an unknown reception and of an unforseen response, and thereby it is in some way 'threatened' ... in the sense that it can become an anonymous ... object of abuse" (TOB 62:3). It "does not at all follow that the human body in its nakedness cannot become the subject of works of art, only that this issue is neither merely aesthetic, nor morally indifferent" (TOB 61:1). It is "connected with a particular responsibility" (TOB 63:4).

> **3b.** There "are works of art whose subject is the human body in its nakedness" which help us see "the whole personal mystery of man. In contact with such works ... in some way we learn the spousal meaning of the body which corresponds to, and provides the measure for 'purity of heart.' But there are also works of art ... that stir up objections ... not because of their object, because in itself the human body always has its own inalienable dignity – but because of the quality or way of its artistic reproduction" (TOB 63:5).

> **3c.** "It seems that Michelangelo, in his own way, allowed himself to be guided by the evocative words of the Book of Genesis which ... reveals: 'The man and his wife were both naked, yet felt no shame (Gen 2:25). *The Sistine Chapel is ... the sanctuary of the theology of the human body.*" For "in the context of the light that comes from God, the human body also keeps its splendor and its dignity. If it is removed from this dimension, it becomes in some way an object, which depreciates very easily, since only before the eyes of God can the human body remain naked and unclothed, and keep its splendor and beauty intact" (*L'Osservatore Romano*, April 13, 1994).

Summary

- For freedom Christ has set us free! True freedom is not liberty to indulge our compulsions, but liberation from our compulsions to indulge. Liberation of the heart from the compulsions of concupiscence is, in fact, the condition of all life together in the truth – for without this liberty, love is impossible.

- Purity of heart enables us to see the human body as God sees it – as a temple of the Holy Spirit and a manifestation of God's own beauty. Blessed are the pure in heart, for they shall see God's mystery revealed *through* the human body.

- Some works of art portray the naked body in a way that helps us to see the "great mystery" of the spousal meaning of the body and the true dignity of the human person. Other portrayals of the body stir objections – not because of their object, because in itself the human body always retains its dignity – but because of the manner it which the body is portrayed.

- We can say that the problem with pornography is not that it reveals too much of the person, but that it reveals far too little. In fact, it's goal is to *obscure the person*, effectively concealing the person's true beauty and mystery.

STUDY QUESTIONS FOR:

SESSION 8: BLESSED ARE THE PURE OF HEART

1. What is "the freedom for which Christ has set us free"? Describe it in your own words.

2. Discuss the difference between freedom as the world understands it and "the freedom for which Christ has set us free."

3. What images, notions, ideas (positive or negative) does the term "purity" conjure up for you?

4. Have you ever heard of purity as the ability to see the mystery of God revealed through the human body in its masculinity and femininity?

5. What does it mean that to the pure all things are pure, but to the impure nothing is pure?

6. St. Paul says that those parts of the body that we (as fallen men) think are "dishonorable" actually deserve "all the greater honor" (1 Co 12:23). If covering the sexual values of the body in public is a virtually universal manifestation of modesty, are we led to do so out of a sense that these parts of our body are "dishonorable"? Or do we cover our sexual values out of a profound sense of "the greater honor" they deserve because of the dignity God bestowed on them? Do we cover our sexual values because we attribute to them an "anti-value," or because we realize they manifest "a value not sufficiently appreciated"? (TOB 45:3).

7. What is the difference between pornography and the naked bodies in the Sistine Chapel?

8. If someone you knew said he was pursuing a career as an artist and his specialty was the naked human body, how would you react?

9. When Hugh Hefner started *Playboy* magazine, where was he right in wanting to portray the naked human body? Where was he wrong?

10. Marriage counselors report that one of today's biggest disruptions to marriage is internet pornography. Why do you think pornography is so damaging to marriage?

CHRIST
APPEALS TO THE
Resurrection

(handwritten) 2/1/10

Session 9
THE ULTIMATE FULFILLMENT
OF THE BODY

1. REVIEW OF PREVIOUS SERIES

Key points from Session Five: *"The Resurrection of the Body"*

- The resurrection of the body is an absolutely essential element of Christian faith. When Christ returns, those who enjoy eternal life will be perfectly integrated, body and soul, as God always intended us to be.

- Marriage is not our be-all and end-all. It is only a sign here on earth that is meant to point us to the "Marriage of the Lamb." We no longer need a sign to point us *to* heaven, when we're *in* heaven.

- In the resurrection, all who respond to the Marriage of the Lamb will be fully divinized – that is, they will participate bodily in God's very nature.

- In the beatific vision, God will give himself totally to man, and man will respond with the total gift of self to God. This eternal communion of glory and bliss was foreshadowed (dimly, of course) right from the beginning in the original unity of man and woman.

- The communion of saints is the unity in "one body" of all who respond to God's wedding invitation. It is the definitive fulfillment of our longing for union with other human beings.

> "THE RESURRECTION OF THE BODY IS ... NOT A DISPENSABLE EXTRA. WHEN DEATH SEPARATES THE TWO WE HAVE A FREAK, A MONSTER, AN OBSCENITY. THAT IS WHY WE ARE TERRIFIED OF GHOSTS AND CORPSES, THOUGH BOTH ARE HARMLESS: THEY ARE THE OBSCENELY SEPARATED ASPECTS OF WHAT BELONGS TOGETHER AS ONE. THAT IS WHY JESUS WEPT AT LAZARUS' GRAVE: NOT MERELY FOR HIS BEREAVEMENT BUT FOR THIS COSMIC OBSCENITY."
>
> – PETER KREEFT

2. THE THIRD "KEY WORD" OF CHRIST

"For in the resurrection they neither marry nor are given in marriage" (Mt 22:30).

- Christ calls us to look in two directions – the beginning and the future.

- Deep in our hearts we experience both an "echo" of the beginning and a premonition of the future.

> **2a.** "As is clear from these words, *marriage* – the union in which ... 'the two will be one flesh' (Gen 2:24) ... belongs *exclusively 'to this world.'*" Yet it is very significant that "Christ reveals the new condition of the human body ... precisely by proposing a reference to and a comparison with the condition in which man shared from the 'beginning'" (TOB 66:2,3).

2b. The absence of marriage in heaven is explained not only by the end of history, but above all by the *authenticity of man's response* to God's 'self-gift. The reciprocal gift of oneself to God – a gift in which man will express all the energies of his humanity, body and soul – will be man's response to God's gift. This exchange will become completely and definitively beatifying (see TOB 68:2-3).

2c. In the resurrection, we will experience a "union with God in his trinitarian mystery and … intimacy with him in the perfect communion of persons" (TOB 67:4). "The eschatological communion of man with God … will be nourished by the vision 'face to face' … of the most perfect communion – because it is purely divine – which is, namely, the *trinitarian communion of the divine Persons* in the unity of the same divinity" (TOB 68:1).

3. Definitive Fulfillment of the Spousal Meaning of the Body

The words of Genesis 2:24 (the two become one flesh) direct us "especially towards this world," but "not completely" (TOB 69:8). These are "sacramental words" and, as such, they point us in some way to the "other world."

- John Paul states several times that we will be raised as males and females, that is, in all the integrity of the maleness and femaleness which originally constituted our individual personhood. Thus, maleness and femaleness will remain an integral part of our communion in heaven.

- Sexual difference and our longing for union reveal that we are created for eternal communion with *the* Eternal Communion: Father, Son, and Holy Spirit.

- The spousal meaning of the body will be fulfilled in an eternal dimension of "incarnate communion" inclusive of all who respond to the wedding invitation of the Lamb.

    3a. In "the resurrection, we discover – in an eschatological perspective – the same characteristics that mark the 'spousal' meaning of the body; we discover them in the encounter with the mystery of the living God … through the face-to-face vision of him" (TOB 67:5).

    3b. "That perennial [spousal] meaning of the human body, to which the existence of every man, burdened by the heritage of concupiscence, has necessarily brought a series of limitations, struggles, and sufferings, will then be revealed again … in [man's] glorified body" (TOB 69:9).

    3c. We can "deduce that the 'spousal' meaning of the body in the resurrection to the future life will perfectly correspond both to the fact that man as male-female is a person, created in the 'image and likeness of God' [recall original solitude], and to the fact that this image is realized in the communion of persons [recall original unity]. That 'spousal' meaning of being a body will, therefore, be realized as a *meaning that is perfectly personal and communitarian at the same time*" (TOB 69:4).

"This … communion of life and love with the Trinity, with the Virgin Mary, the angels and all the blessed – is called 'heaven.' Heaven is the ultimate end and fulfillment of the deepest human longings, the state of supreme, definitive happiness."

– *Catechism of the Catholic Church* (1024)

3d. The "virginal state of the body will manifest itself completely as the eschatological fulfillment of the 'spousal' meaning of the body" (TOB 68:3). Heaven will be the experience "of both perpetual 'virginity' (united with the spousal meaning of the body) and perpetual 'intersubjectivity' of all human begins who will share (as males and females) in the resurrection" (TOB 71:5).

3e. In the "eschatological 'virginity' of the risen man ... the absolute and eternal spousal meaning of the glorified body will be revealed in union with God himself, by seeing him 'face to face." The body will be "glorified moreover through the union of a perfect intersubjectivity that will unite all the 'sharers in the other world,' men and women, in the mystery of the communion of saints" (TOB 75:1).

4. St. Paul's Interpretation of the Resurrection

The First Adam and the Last Adam

"'The first man, Adam, became a living being'; the last Adam became a life-giving spirit ... As we have borne the image of the man of earth, so we will bear the image of the man of heaven" (1 Co 15:45, 49).

- Within history, man lives in a "tension between the two poles" of the first and last Adam.

- This tension awakens a great hope, akin to a woman's labor pains (see Rom 8:23).

- The body is in "bondage to decay" (Rom 8:21). It is destined to "return to dust" (Gen 3:19), but also to be re-quickened by the life-giving spirit ("breath") of the last Adam.

  4a. The resurrection is not merely "a return to the state the soul shared in before sin." That would "not correspond to the inner logic of the whole economy of salvation, to the deepest meaning of the mystery of redemption." The resurrection "can only be *an introduction to a new fullness* ... that presupposes man's whole history, formed by the drama of the tree of the knowledge of good and evil" (TOB 72:3).

  4b. "The humanity of the 'first Adam,' the 'man of earth,' carries within itself ... *a particular potentiality* (which is capacity and readiness) *for receiving* all *that the 'second Adam' became,* the heavenly Man, namely, Christ: what he became in his resurrection" (TOB 71:3).

  4c. Humanity "carries within itself the desire for glory" (TOB 71:3) because "everyone bears in himself the image of Adam [who] is also called to bear in himself the image of Christ, the image of the risen One" (TOB 71:4).

  4d. "The truth is that only in the mystery of incarnate Word does the mystery of man take on light ... Christ, the final Adam ... fully reveals man to himself and makes his supreme calling clear" (GS 22).

"As we learn from Christ's words about the resurrection, the union of the sexes as we know it now will give way to an *infinitely greater* union. Those who are raised in glory will experience a bliss so far superior to earthly sexual union that our wee brains can't even begin to imagine it. Eye has not seen, ear has not heard, nor has it even dawned on us what God has prepared for those who love him (see 1 Cor 2:9)."

– From *Theology of the Body for Beginners*

- Christ says that in the resurrection we will not be given in marriage. This absence of marriage is explained not only by the end of history, but above all by the ultimate relationship of love between God and Man. This exchange will fulfill every hunger and ache for love and union beyond our wildest imaginings.

- Sexual difference reveals that we are created for eternal communion with *the* Eternal Communion: Father, Son, and Holy Spirit. In the eschatological reality, the spousal meaning of the body will be lived through our glorified masculinity and femininity in union with God himself, by seeing him "face to face."

- Within history, man lives in a "tension between the two poles" of the first and last Adam. This tension awakens a great hope, akin to a woman's labor pains, a hope for eternal glory. Everyone bears in himself the image of Adam, and we are all destined to become what Christ became in his resurrection.

STUDY QUESTIONS FOR:

SESSION 9: THE ULTIMATE FULFILLMENT OF THE BODY

1. What does it mean that there will not be marriage in heaven?

2. Why do you think so many people are saddened to learn that there will not be marriage in heaven?

3. What happens to the sexual relationship when we lose sight of our ultimate destiny in heaven?

4. Will there be sex in heaven?

5. How will the "Marriage of the Lamb" fulfill the spousal meaning of our bodies as male and female?

6. What does it mean to say that our experience of the spousal meaning of the body will be a "virginal" experience in heaven?

7. Why do you think so many people – including many Christians – have a disembodied view of the afterlife?

8. John Paul II says we all have a God-given "desire for glory." Do you sense this within yourself? How does it manifest itself?

9. How has our "desire for glory" become twisted as a result of original sin? What is the solution?

> #### DEAR FATHER, SON, AND HOLY SPIRIT,
> *You live a life of eternal bliss in self-giving love. You created me to share in that love, to share in your own bliss forever in heaven. Forgive me for ever doubting your gift. Forgive me for all the ways I grasp at happiness, pleasure, comfort. Forgive me for all the ways I try to satisfy the hungers of my heart on my own rather than believing in your gift to me, rather than opening my desire to you and trusting in you to fulfill it. Jesus, I thirst. Bring me to the waters of life. Jesus, I hunger. Feed me with the bread of eternal life. Jesus, I yearn for the ecstasy for which you created me. Intoxicate me with your sweet wine now and forever. Amen.*

4/16

9/20

> "CHRISTIAN REVELATION RECOGNIZES TWO SPECIFIC WAYS OF REALIZING THE VOCATION OF THE HUMAN PERSON, IN ITS ENTIRETY, TO LOVE: MARRIAGE AND VIRGINITY OR CELIBACY. EITHER ONE IS IN ITS OWN PROPER FORM AN ACTUATION OF THE MOST PROFOUND TRUTH ABOUT MAN, OF HIS BEING 'CREATED IN THE IMAGE OF GOD' [AS MALE AND FEMALE]."
>
> –POPE JOHN PAUL II

1. REVIEW OF PREVIOUS SERIES

Key points from Session Six: *"Celibacy for the Kingdom"*

- Which marriage provides ultimate fulfillment – the marriage of Genesis (man and woman), or the marriage of Revelation (Christ and the Church)? Those who are celibate for the sake of the Kingdom share the same vocation to love as those who marry, but they manifest this same vocation in a different manner.

- Christian celibacy is *not* a rejection of sexuality. Rather, it is meant to be a living out of the ultimate purpose and meaning of sexuality – union with Christ and the Church. The celibate person must embrace the spousal meaning of his or her body and live it in an authentic call to union and spiritual fertility.

- Celibacy is not a life of sexual repression but of sexual redemption. Christ calls everyone to experience liberation from lust through the redemption of the body. Only to the degree that one is free from the domination of lust is he or she able to live a healthy life either as a married person or as a celibate.

2. CHRIST'S INVITATION

A New Way of Understanding the Body

"For there are eunuchs who have been so from birth, and there are eunuchs who have been made eunuchs by men, and there are eunuchs who have made themselves eunuchs for the sake of the kingdom of heaven" (Mt 19:12).

> **2a.** It is as if Christ were saying, "I know that what I am going to tell you now will raise great difficulties in your consciousness, in your way of understanding the meaning of the body; I shall speak to you, in fact, about continence, and this will undoubtedly be associated in you with a state of physical deficiency, inborn or acquired by human cause. I want to tell you, by contrast, that continence can also be voluntary and chosen by man 'for the kingdom of heaven'" (TOB 74:4).

2b. In order "to clarify what the kingdom of heaven is for those who choose voluntary continence for its sake, *the revelation of the spousal relationship between Christ and the Church* has particular significance" (TOB 79:7).

Fruitfulness from the Spirit

"Joseph, son of David, do not fear to take Mary as your wife because that which is conceived in her is of the Holy Spirit" (Mt 1:20).

- The virginal-marriage of Joseph and Mary embraces the heavenly marriage and the earthly marriage *simultaneously*. In turn, their virginal marriage literally effected the marriage of heaven and earth.

- All men and women who live an authentic life of celibacy "for the kingdom" participate in some way in this superabundant fruitfulness.

2c. "Mary and Joseph ... became the first witnesses of a fruitfulness different from that of the flesh, that is, the fruitfulness of the Spirit: 'What is begotten in her comes from the Holy Spirit' (Mt 1:20)" (TOB 75:2).

2d. "*The marriage of Mary with Joseph ... conceals within itself,* at the same time, *the mystery* of the perfect communion of persons, of Man and Woman in the conjugal covenant and at the same time the mystery of this *singular 'continence for the kingdom of heaven'*: a continence that served the most perfect *'fruitfulness of the Holy Spirit'* in the history of salvation. Indeed, it was in some way the absolute fullness of that spiritual fruitfulness, because precisely in ... Mary and Joseph's covenant in marriage and continence, the gift of the Incarnation of the Eternal Word was realized" (TOB 75:3).

2e. Christian celibacy "must lead in its normal development to 'fatherhood' or 'motherhood' in the spiritual sense ... in a way analogous to conjugal love" (TOB 78:5).

2f. Although Christ "is born from her like every man ... still Mary's motherhood was virginal; and to this virginal motherhood corresponded the virginal mystery of Joseph" (TOB 75:2).

2g. "The difficulty of accepting the sublime mystery of their spousal communion has led some, since the second century, to think of Joseph as advanced in age and to consider him Mary's guardian more than her husband. It is instead a case of supposing that he was not an elderly man at the time, but that his interior perfection, the fruit of grace, led him to live his spousal relationship with Mary with virginal affection" (TT, p. 128).

2h. "*In this family, Joseph is the father: his fatherhood* is not one that derives from begetting offspring; but neither is it an 'apparent' or merely 'substitute' fatherhood. Rather, it is one that *fully shares in authentic human fatherhood*" (RC 21).

"FOR ALL CHRIST'S FAITHFUL RELIGIOUS RECALL THAT WONDERFUL MARRIAGE MADE BY GOD, WHICH WILL BE FULLY MANIFESTED IN THE FUTURE AGE, AND IN WHICH THE CHURCH HAS CHRIST FOR HER ONLY SPOUSE."

– SECOND VATICAN COUNCIL

Seminary
Priest – Fr.
spiritual

Bishop Sheen
Virginal
Perfection
of union
This is my
body given for
you –
authentic
Christian community

"BLESSED BE ... YOUR MOST PURE WOMB THAT WAS FOUND DESERVING TO BE THE TABERNACLE OF THE DIVINITY ... BLESSED BE YOUR HOLY BREASTS, WHICH FED THE ONE WHO MAINTAINS AND SUSTAINS THE ENTIRE UNIVERSE WITH THE SWEET NECTAR OF YOU MOST PURE BLOOD!"

– SOR JUANA INES DE LA CRUZ (17TH CENTURY)

3. COMPLEMENTARITY OF MARRIAGE AND CELIBACY

Marriage and celibacy do not conflict. They're meant to "explain or complete each other" (TOB 78:2).

- Marriage reveals the spousal character of the celibate vocation just as the celibate vocation reveals the sacramentality of marriage.

- Celibacy for the kingdom is a "sign," but it is not a sacrament. Rather, it anticipates the life *beyond* sacraments.

    3a. "In the life of an authentically Christian community, the attitudes and the values proper to the one and the other state ... *complete each other and in some sense interpenetrate.*" For "the nature of the one as well as the other love is 'spousal,' that is, expressed through the complete gift of self" (TOB 78:4).

    3b. Christian celibacy is indispensable for the clearer recognition of the value of marriage and family life. Renouncing marriage for the kingdom *is at the same time a particular form of affirmation of the value* of marriage. This may seem like a paradox. We know, however, that paradox goes hand in hand with many statements of the Gospel (see TOB 81:3,6).

    3c. Both vocations "provide a full answer to one of man's underlying questions: namely, the question about the meaning of 'being a body,' that is, the meaning of masculinity and femininity, of being ... a man or a woman" (TOB 85:9).

    3d. "In order for man to be fully *aware of what he is choosing* (continence for the kingdom), he must also be fully aware *of what he is renouncing*" (TOB 81:2).

4. CONCLUSION OF PART I (THE WORDS OF CHRIST)

Redemption of the Body and "the Hope of Everyday"

The *ethos of redemption* is "more precisely, the ethos of the redemption of the body" (TOB 49:2). We "groan inwardly as we wait for ... the redemption of our bodies" (Rom 8:23).

- The redemption of the body is the ultimate point of arrival in the TOB, the end that determines all the steps we are taking in this study (see TOB, p. 110).

- In fact, the phrase "theology of the body" is in some way synonymous with the phrase "redemption of the body" (see TOB, p. 111).

    4a. The "'redemption of the body' ... expresses itself not only in the resurrection as victory over death. It is present also in the words of Christ addressed to 'historical' man [when] Christ invites us to overcome concupiscence, even in the exclusively inner movements of the human heart" (TOB 86:6).

4b. "The 'redemption of the body' … expresses itself not only in … the eschatological hope of the resurrection, but [also in] the hope of victory over sin, which can be called the hope of everyday. In his everyday life, man must draw from the mystery of the redemption of the body the inspiration and strength to overcome the evil that is dormant in him in the form of the threefold concupiscence" (TOB 86:6-7).

4c. "Everything we have tried to do in the course of our meditations in order to understand the words of Christ has its definitive foundation in the mystery of the redemption of the body" (TOB 86:8).

Soul of Christ, sanctify me
Body of Christ, save me
Blood of Christ, inebriate me
Water from Christ's side, wash me
Passion of Christ, strengthen me
O good Jesus, hear me
Within your wounds hide me
Suffer me not to be separated from you
From the malicious enemy defend me
In the hour of my death call me
And bid me come to you
That I may praise you with the saints
and with the angels
Forever and ever
Amen.

Summary

- All men and women who live an authentic life of celibacy "for the kingdom" participate in a very particular way in the spousal relationship of Christ and the Church. They also share in a very particular way in the superabundant fruitfulness of this relationship.

- The virginal-marriage of Joseph and Mary embraces the heavenly marriage and the earthly marriage *simultaneously*. In turn, their virginal marriage literally effected the marriage of heaven and earth. In this way, Mary and Joseph became the first witnesses of a fruitfulness different from that of the flesh, that is, the fruitfulness of the Holy Spirit.

- Marriage and celibacy do not conflict. They're meant to explain or complete each other. Marriage reveals the spousal character of the celibate vocation just as the celibate vocation reveals the sacramentality of marriage. Both loves are "spousal" in as much as they are expressed through the unreserved gift of oneself.

- Everything we have studied in the TOB has its definitive foundation in the mystery of the redemption of the body. The redemption of the body expresses itself not only in the final hope of the resurrection, but also in the hope of victory over sin in the here and now. This can be called "the hope of everyday."

STUDY QUESTIONS FOR:
SESSION 10: CELIBACY AND SEXUALITY

1. Why do we call a priest "father"? Why is the superior of a women's religious order called "mother"? Why are religious called "brother" and "sister"?

2. Many people grow up with the impression that Mary was "too holy" to have sexual relations with Joseph, as if sex itself is somehow inherently "unholy." Did you have such an impression? Discuss.

3. What is the root of this error – that is, considering sexual relations to be inherently suspect or "unholy."

4. Why do you think this error can so easily creep into our thinking? Do you think there is an element of truth in this error? If so, what is it?

5. John Paul II speaks of the "difficulty" of accepting the "sublime mystery" of Joseph and Mary's love. What makes it difficult?

6. Joseph is described by Catholic prayer and piety as Mary's "most chaste spouse." What does that expression conjure up in your mind? In light of what you are learning in your study of TOB, what does it mean to be a "most chaste spouse"?

7. Explain in your own words how celibacy and marriage "explain and complete each other."

8. What practical steps can you take in your parish to demonstrate the inter-relationship of marriage and celibacy for the kingdom?

9. John Paul says that the "redemption of the body" is not only reserved for the end of time when our bodies are raised, but also concerns the hope of overcoming concupiscence in the here and now. Can you point to an experience in your life that demonstrates this "hope of every day"?

THE GRACE
OF THE
Sacrament

10/26

> "ST. JOHN CHRYSOSTOM SUGGESTS THAT YOUNG HUSBANDS SHOULD SAY TO THEIR WIVES: I HAVE TAKEN YOU IN MY ARMS, AND I LOVE YOU, AND PREFER YOU TO MY LIFE ITSELF. FOR THE PRESENT LIFE IS NOTHING, AND MY MOST ARDENT DREAM IS TO SPEND IT WITH YOU IN SUCH A WAY THAT WE MAY BE ASSURED OF NOT BEING SEPARATED IN THE LIFE RESERVED FOR US."
>
> – *CATECHISM OF THE CATHOLIC CHURCH* (2365)

1. REVIEW OF PREVIOUS SERIES

Key points from Session Seven: *"Marriage as a Sacrament"*

- Ephesians 5 does *not* justify male domination. Rather, it calls husbands to love their wives "as Christ loved the Church." Christ came not to be served, but to serve.

- When understood in its proper context, "Wives, submit to your husbands" actually means "Wives, allow your husbands to *serve you*."

- Marriage is not only one of the seven sacraments, but a model of all of the sacraments. The goal of all of the sacraments is to unite the Bridegroom (Christ) and the Bride (the Church) and to fill the Church with divine life.

2. THE TEXT OF EPHESIANS 5

"Be subject to one another out of reverence for Christ. Wives, be subject to your husbands, as to the Lord. For the husband is the head of the wife as Christ is the head of the church, his body, and is himself its Savior. As the church is subject to Christ, so let wives also be subject in everything to their husbands. Husbands, love your wives, as Christ loved the church and gave himself up for her, that he might sanctify her, having cleansed her by the washing of water with the word, that he might present the church to himself in splendor, without spot or wrinkle or any such thing, that she might be holy and without blemish. Even so husbands should love their wives as their own bodies. He who loves his wife loves himself. For no man ever hates his own flesh, but nourishes and cherishes it, as Christ does the church, because we are members of his body. 'For this reason a man shall leave his father and mother and be joined to his wife, and the two shall become one flesh.' This is a great mystery, and I mean in reference to Christ and the church; however, let each one of you love his wife as himself, and let the wife see that she respects her husband" (Eph 5:21-33).

The Crowning of the Truths of Scripture

The above "key and classic text" takes us to the threshold of the meaning and mystery of the universe, to the threshold of discovering the glory and greatness that God has bestowed on us by creating us as male and female and calling us to become "one flesh."

- It isn't coincidental that in our day this passage is often vehemently contested.

- Here we glimpse a great clash of two competing anthropologies (or humanisms) and their respective views of the human body and the meaning of sexuality.

- Nor is it coincidental that this passage is followed by the call to take up arms in the great "spiritual battle": Gird your loins with the truth! (see Eph 6:14)

    2a. "Saint Paul's magnificent synthesis concerning the 'great mystery' appears as the compendium or *summa*, in some sense, *of the teaching about God and man* which was brought to fulfillment by Christ" (LF 19).

    2b. We should consider this passage "as the 'crowning' of the themes and that ebb and flow like long waves through the Word of God revealed in Sacred Scripture" (TOB 87:3). The "great mystery" of Ephesians 5 "is what God … wishes above all to transmit to mankind in his Word" (TOB 93:2).

    2c. "In the letter to the Ephesians, we are witnesses … of a particular encounter of [the divine] mystery with the very essence of the vocation to marriage" (TOB 89:7).

    2d. We must try to "understand if possible 'to the very depths' what wealth of truth revealed by God is contained within the scope of that stupendous page. Using the well-known expression of … *Gaudium et Spes,* one can say that [this] passage … 'reveals —in a particular way— *man to man himself* and makes *his supreme vocation* clear' (GS 22)" (TOB 87:6).

    2e. "One must recognize the logic of this wonderful text, which radically frees our way of thinking from Manichaean elements" (TOB 117b:2).

3. SACRAMENT AND MYSTERY

"Sacrament" – in the more ancient, broader meaning of the word – refers to the revelation of the mystery hidden in God. "Mystery" is the only word we can utter to speak of the divine reality.

- Together, these words – "mystery-sacrament" – refer to the "hidden-revealed" dimensions of God and his plan for humanity.

> "THE HUMAN LOVE OF ENGAGED COUPLES, OF SPOUSES, AND OF FATHERS AND MOTHERS … IS A BIG SUBJECT THAT I NEVER CEASE TO EXAMINE, AND I SEE MORE AND MORE CLEARLY HOW DEEPLY IT IS INSCRIBED IN THE WORDS OF CHRISTIAN REVELATION. I THINK THERE IS MUCH TO BE DONE IN THIS FIELD. THE SITUATION IN THE CHURCH AND IN THE WORLD IN THIS RESPECT IS A CHALLENGE."
>
> – POPE JOHN PAUL II

- Sacraments reveal spiritual mysteries through physical signs. Sign simply means the "visibility of the Invisible" (see TOB 95b:7).

- The *good news* of the Gospel is that that which was *hidden* in God from eternity has been *revealed* – first through "the sign" of man and woman's original unity (sacrament of creation) and *definitively* through "the sign" of the union of Christ and the Church (sacrament of redemption).

  3a. "The sacrament consists in *'manifesting'* [the divine] *mystery in a sign* that serves not only to proclaim the mystery but also *to accomplish it* in man." But "even after its proclamation (or revelation) it does not cease to be called 'mystery'" (TOB 93:5).

  3b. "By presenting the relationship of Christ with the Church according to the image of the spousal union of husband and wife, [the Apostle] speaks ... about the way in which [the divine] *mystery* ... has *become visible* and thereby *entered into the sphere of the Sign*" (TOB 95b:6).

  3c. The linking of the "one flesh" union with the union of Christ and the Church "is the most important point of the whole text, *in some sense its keystone*" (TOB 93:1). "It is a particular merit of the author of Ephesians that he brought these two signs together, making of them *the single great sign,* that is, *a great sacrament*"(TOB 95b:7).

  3d. "One can say that the visible sign of marriage 'in the beginning,' inasmuch as it is linked to the visible sign of Christ and the Church on the summit of God's saving economy, *transposes* the eternal plan of love *into the 'historical' dimension* and makes it *the foundation of the whole sacramental order*" (TOB 95b:7).

The Sacrament of Creation (Primordial Sacrament)

If sacraments communicate the grace of Christ, how can we speak of a "sacrament" before Christ's coming? The Father "chose us in [Christ] before the foundation of the world" (Eph 1:3-4).

- The Incarnation should not be considered "plan B." God's *eternal* plan is that Christ would "leave his Father" and be joined to his bride in one flesh (Incarnation). Sin cannot and did not thwart this plan.

- Recall our reflections on "Knowledge and Procreation": God's original plan continues even after sin, and is directed toward the fullness of redemption – it awaits the New Eve who will "bear a child with the help of the Lord" (see Gen 4:1).

  3e. "Before sin ... man carried in his soul the fruit of eternal election in Christ ... Through [this] grace ... man, male and female, was 'holy and immaculate' before God [as demonstrated] in the fact that, though both were 'naked ... they did not feel shame' (Gen 2:25)." This grace "was given in view of [Christ] ... although – according to the dimensions of time and history – it preceded the Incarnation" (TOB 96:4,5).

"CREATION ... CULMINATES IN CHRIST. CONVERSELY, THE MYSTERY OF CHRIST CASTS CONCLUSIVE LIGHT ON THE MYSTERY OF CREATION AND REVEALS THE END FOR WHICH 'IN THE BEGINNING GOD CREATED THE HEAVENS AND THE EARTH': FROM THE BEGINNING, GOD ENVISAGED THE GLORY OF THE NEW CREATION IN CHRIST."

– CATECHISM OF THE CATHOLIC CHURCH (280)

3f. "Redemption was to become the source of man's supernatural endowment after sin and, in a certain sense, despite sin. This supernatural endowment, which took place before original sin … was brought about precisely *out of regard for [Christ]* … while chronologically anticipating his coming in the body" (TOB 96:5).

The Sacrament of Redemption (Definitive Sacrament)

The one flesh union "is a great mystery, and I mean in reference to Christ and the church" (Eph 5:21-33).

- Marital love and union is the original pattern that gives shape to the whole mystery of our redemption.

- All of the seven sacraments bear the mark of the "one and only sacrament" (see TOB 98:3) of the beginning (marriage).

  3g. The "sacrament of redemption clothes itself, so to speak, in the figure and form of the primordial sacrament. To the marriage of the first husband and wife … corresponds the marriage, or rather the analogy of the marriage, of Christ with the Church" (TOB 97:2).

  3h. The "Mystery hidden from all eternity in God … in the sacrament of creation became *a visible reality through the union* of the first man and woman in … marriage." This same mystery "becomes in the sacrament of redemption *a visible reality in the indissoluble union of Christ with the Church*, which the author of Ephesians presents as the spousal union" (TOB 97:4).

  3i. "The entire Christian life bears the mark of the spousal love of Christ and the Church. Already Baptism … is a nuptial mystery; it is so to speak the nuptial bath which precedes the wedding feast, the Eucharist" (CCC 1617).

"REVELATION, AS MANIFEST IN SCRIPTURE AND … TRADITION … PROPOSES THE NUPTIAL MYSTERY AS THE KEY FOR UNDERSTANDING (BY ANALOGY, OF COURSE) THE SALIENT ASPECTS, THE DOGMA, OF OUR FAITH."

– ANGELO CARDINAL SCOLA

Summary

- Saint Paul's magnificent synthesis concerning the "great mystery" in Ephesians 5 serves as a concise summary of the entire teaching about God and man which was brought to fulfillment by Christ. The "great mystery" of Ephesians 5 is what God wishes above all to transmit to mankind in his Word.

- In as much as marital union is linked to the union of Christ and the Church, it serves as the foundation of the whole sacramental order, pointing us toward the summit of that order – the Eucharist. It is a particular merit of St. Paul that he brought these two signs together, making of them *one great sign*.

- The Incarnation should not be considered "plan B." God's *eternal* plan is that Christ would "leave his Father" and be joined to his bride in one flesh (Incarnation). Sin cannot and did not thwart this plan. Grace in Christ was given to man *before* sin while chronologically anticipating his coming in the body.

- Marital union is the original pattern that gives shape to the whole mystery of our redemption. The eternal mystery was revealed in the "sacrament of creation" *through the spousal union* of the first man and woman. This same mystery is revealed in "the sacrament of redemption" *through the spousal union* of Christ with the Church.

STUDY QUESTIONS FOR:

SESSION 11: THE "GREAT MYSTERY" OF MARRIAGE

1. Explain why you think there is so much controversy over Ephesians 5. Why do you think people immediately jump to conclusions about the meaning of "submission" without reading this in context?

2. Explain in your own words why the "great mystery" of Ephesians 5 (where Paul links the union of spouses with the union of Christ and the Church) serves as a summary of the entire message and teaching of the Bible.

3. Did you grow up learning that the "one flesh" union is meant to be a great foreshadowing of the eternal joy and ecstasy that awaits us in heaven? If not, what impression about sex did you gain from your parents, from your religion teachers, from your parish priests?

4. John Paul calls the visible sign of marriage "the foundation of the whole sacramental order." Theologians will be unpacking this statement for centuries, but what does it mean, practically speaking? What difference does or should this make in our day to day lives?

5. Does the idea that the Incarnation is not "plan B" change your understanding of Christianity? If so, how?

6. How does marriage become the "pattern" by which the mystery of redemption is shaped? Where do we see this, practically speaking, in the Church's life of faith?

7. How does the "marital shape" of Christianity help answer controversial questions such as a male-only priesthood, so-called gay "marriage," etc.?

8. How can the truths I'm learning be brought into my own personal life of prayer?

SPOUSAL AND REDEMPTIVE LOVE

1. MARRIAGE AND THE "REDEMPTION OF THE BODY"

The Sacrament – Call to Embrace the Good News of the Gospel

The Gospel reveals that redemptive grace has been poured into the very depths of the human heart enabling men and women, whatever their weaknesses and sins, to respond to the call to marriage just as it was instituted "in the beginning" and as St. Paul exhorts in Ephesians 5.

> **1a.** "Christ … *opens* marriage to the salvific action of God, *to the powers flowing 'from the redemption of the body,'* which help to overcome the consequences of sin and to build the unity of man and woman according to the Creator's eternal plan" (TOB 100:2).

> **1b.** By "following Christ, renouncing themselves, and taking up their crosses … spouses will be able to 'receive' the original meaning of marriage and live it with the help of Christ" (CCC 1615).

> **1c.** The sacrament of marriage is *"an exhortation* addressed to man, *male and female, that they might conscientiously share in the redemption of the body."* Historical man "must find again the dignity and holiness of conjugal union … on the basis of the mystery of redemption" (TOB 100:4,6).

The Sacrament – Call to "Life According to the Spirit"

It is the Holy Spirit who empowers spouses to live the Christian ethos of marriage. As much as lust distorts the human heart, even more so does the Holy Spirit transform and revive it.

> **1d.** "As a sacrament … marriage is an efficacious expression of the saving power of God." Through the redemption of the body, *"one can master the concupiscence of the flesh …* [that] tendency toward an egotistical satisfaction, and in the sacramental covenant of masculinity and femininity, 'flesh' itself becomes the specific 'substratum' of a lasting and indissoluble communion of persons … in a manner worthy of persons" (TOB 101:1,4).

> **1e.** "Just as 'concupiscence' darkens the horizon of interior vision and deprives hearts of the lucid clarity of desires and aspirations, so 'life according to the Spirit' … allows man and woman to find again the true freedom of the gift together with the awareness of the spousal meaning of the body" (TOB 101:5).

"WE, WHO LIVE IN A COUNTRY STILL INFLUENCED BY PURITANISM, EVEN IF ONLY IN REACTION AGAINST IT, HAVE MUCH NEED TO BE CONVINCED OF THE TRUE GOODNESS OF OUR BODIES AND ESPECIALLY OF OUR OWN SEXUALITY. AT TIMES WHAT PREVENTS THIS CONVICTION IS THAT WE FEAR OUR SEXUALITY BECAUSE OF ITS VIOLENCE AND THE EASE WITH WHICH IT CAN GET OUT OF CONTROL; WE SENSE ITS CONNECTION WITH ORIGINAL SIN AND OUR OWN ACTUAL SINS … AT OTHER TIMES, WE DESPISE OUR SEXUAL POWERS BECAUSE … WE FIND PLEASURE IN THEM BUT NO SENSE OF TRUE MEANING, SIGNIFICANCE, OR HUMAN WORTH. BUT WE FORGET, WHEN WE ARE AFRAID OF OUR SEXUALITY, THAT THE BEST PROTECTION FROM SIN IN THIS MATTER IS TO REVERE AND ESTEEM OUR SEXUALITY AS GOD REVERES AND ESTEEMS IT."

– FR. PAUL QUAY S.J.

1f. Spouses "are called to chastity as … life 'according to the Spirit'" (TOB 101:4). "Thus, life 'according to the Spirit' expresses itself also in the reciprocal 'union' … by which … they become 'one flesh'" (TOB 101:6).

1g. If sexual union is to be "according to the Spirit," spouses must trustingly "submit their masculinity and femininity to the blessing of procreation … Here too, *life 'according to the Spirit'* … expresses itself in *the deep awareness of the holiness of the life* … to which both [may] give rise, thereby participating in the powers of the mystery of creation" (TOB 101:6).

1h. "And if 'the whole of creation groans and suffers until now in labor pains' (Rom 8:22), a particular hope accompanies the mother's labor pains, namely, the hope of the 'revelation of the sons of God,' a hope which every newborn who comes into the world carries a spark within himself" (TOB 101:6).

The Sacrament – Call to Live Forever

Lust "is not of the Father but is of the world" (1 Jn 2:16). However, John Paul II tells us that marriage, including the sexual love proper to spouses, is not "of the world" but "of the Father." The lust of the world "passes away … but he who does the will of God lives forever" (1 Jn 2:17).

- Deep in the human heart a battle rages for dominance between that which is "of the Father" and that which is "of the world." A battle rages between love and lust, between hope and despondency, between life and all that opposes it.

- Genesis tells us with certainty that fertility is a blessing from the Father (see Gen 1:28). Tragically, after the fall, we are often led to consider it a curse.

- Here we can see that the blessing of fertility forces us to choose between that which is "of the Father" and that which is "of the world." And this choice literally has eternal consequences.

- Fertility is an affirmation of "life" – not only temporal life, but *eternal life.* Eternal life literally comes to us through a woman's yes to "life according to the Spirit": our earthly mother's and Mary, our Blessed Mother.

  1i. The grace of "marriage as a sacrament immutably serves the purpose that man, male and female, by mastering concupiscence, does the will of the Father. And the one who 'does the will of God will remain in eternity' (1 Jn 2:17). In this sense, marriage as a sacrament also bears within itself the germ of man's eschatological future" (TOB 101:10-11).

  1j. "Chastity is a promise of immortality" (CCC 2347).

> "THE WORD INSCRIBED IN THE BODY … SPEAKS OF THE OTHER; IT SPEAKS OF GOD, OR WHAT IS HOLY … SEXUALITY MARKS OUR BODY WITH THE SIGN OF THIS SPLENDID PLAN: I AM GOD'S PARTNER; GOD IS MY OWN IDENTITY."
>
> – CARLO CARDINAL MARTINI

2. THE SPOUSAL AND REDEMPTIVE MEANING OF THE BODY

The spousal meaning of the body expressed in the union of the first Adam and Eve takes on a redemptive meaning in the union of the New Adam and Eve (Christ and the Church).

- The spousal meaning of the body reveals that we are called to love as God loves. However, this side of original sin, we cannot fulfill this without experiencing the redemption of the body.

- The redemption of the body is accomplished when the New Adam fulfills the spousal meaning of his body, becoming a "sincere gift" to his Bride on the Cross ("It is consummated," see Jn 19:30).

> **2a.** "The Pauline image of marriage ... brings together the redemptive dimension of love with its spousal dimension. In some sense it unites these two dimensions [into] one. Christ ... has married the Church as his bride because 'he gave himself for her' (Eph 5:25). Through marriage as a sacrament ... *both of these dimensions of love, the spousal and the redemptive* ... penetrate into the life of the spouses" (TOB 102:4).

> **2b.** The "'great mystery' of Christ's union with the Church obliges us to link *the spousal meaning of the body with its redemptive meaning*." This link "is important with regard to marriage and to the Christian vocation of husbands and wives." However it "is equally essential and *valid for the [understanding] of man* in general: for the fundamental problem of understanding him and for the self-understanding of his being in the world." Indeed, it is in this link that we "find the answer to the question about the meaning of 'being a body'" (TOB 102:5).

> **2c.** "Man, who is 'from the beginning' male and female, must seek the meaning of his existence and the meaning of his humanity by reaching all the way to the mystery of creation through the reality of redemption ... The union of Christ with the Church allows us to understand in what way the spousal meaning of the body is completed by the redemptive meaning ... [and] not only in marriage." This happens on all "the different roads of life and in different situations ... indeed, in man's very *birth and death*" (TOB 102:8).

> **2d.** The redemptive and spousal love of Christ for the Church embraces "every human being and, in some sense, everything created, as the Pauline text on the 'redemption of the body' indicates" ("the whole of creation has been groaning in travail"). "Through the 'great mystery' discussed in Ephesians ... marriage is inscribed anew in the 'sacrament of man,' which embraces the universe." This "sacrament of man and of the world ... is formed according to the model of the spousal love of Christ and the Church, until the measure of the definitive fulfillment is reached in the kingdom of the Father" (TOB 102:7, 8).

"The Spirit and the Bride say, 'Come'" (Rev 22:17). Come, Lord Jesus, open our minds and our hearts to the "great mystery" hidden in the depths of God from all eternity (see Eph 3:9). Give us the eyes to see an image of this "great mystery" in our creation as male and female and in our call to become "one body" in marital communion (see Gen 2:24). Give us the eyes to see the definitive revelation of this "great mystery" in our redemption as male and female and in our call to become "one body" with you in Eucharistic Communion (see Eph 5:31-32). Plant deep within our breast an abiding hope in the resurrection of our bodies, when all who respond to the wedding invitation (see Mt 22:1-14) will behold you face to face, and know you in the eternal consummation of the "Marriage of the Lamb" (see Rev 19:7).

Summary

- Redemption empowers men and women, whatever their weaknesses and sins, to respond to the call to marriage just as it was instituted "in the beginning" and as St. Paul exhorts in Ephesians 5. As much as lust distorts the human heart, even more so does the Holy Spirit transform and revive it.

- Fertility forces us to choose between that which is "of the Father" and that which is "of the world." Fertility is an affirmation not only of temporal life, but of *eternal life*. For those who do the will of the Father live forever. In this way, a chaste marriage becomes a promise of immortality.

- The "great mystery" of Ephesians 5 obliges us to link the *spousal meaning of our bodies* with the mystery of the *redemption of our bodies*. This link is obviously important with regard to marriage. However it is equally essential for everyone. It is in this link that we discover the very meaning of our existence, the very meaning of our life, birth, and death.

- The redemptive and spousal love of Christ for the Church embraces every human being and even reaches to the furthest ends of the universe. All of creation is groaning in travail awaiting the consummation of the spousal love of Christ and the Church, until the measure of the definitive fulfillment is reached in the kingdom of the Father.

STUDY QUESTIONS FOR:
SESSION 12: SPOUSAL AND REDEMPTIVE LOVE

1. Bill has fought a pornography/masturbation addiction since he was a teenager. Sally, his wife of 22 years, has had multiple affairs. Is there hope for this couple to have a marriage that truly reflects the love of Christ for the Church?

2. Trace the practical steps that Bill and Sally might take in order to begin "entering into" the great mystery of marriage as unfolded in the TOB.

3. We've learned that becoming "one flesh" is meant to be an expression of "life according to the Spirit." What does this mean, practically speaking, for Bill and Sally?

4. Bill got a vasectomy after Sally gave birth to their second child. Sally agreed that it was a good idea. What role, if any, do you think this decision has played in their difficulties?

5. What does it mean to say chastity is a pledge of immortality?

6. It is obvious that linking the "one flesh" union with the union of Christ and the Church is important for a Christian understanding of marriage. But John Paul II claims this is "equally essential" for everyone, for understanding the very meaning of human life. Why would this be so?

7. What does it mean to say that the "great mystery" of Christ's spousal love for the Church goes beyond humanity and in some way "embraces the universe"?

8. Does Christ's "spousal love" for all of creation have any practical importance? Does it or should it make a difference in the way I live my day to day life? What implications might it have, say, for the way we treat the environment?

THE SIGN
OF THE
Sacrament

Session 13
THE LANGUAGE OF THE BODY

1/16/11

1. REVIEW OF PREVIOUS SERIES

Key points from Sessions Seven and Eight

The body has a "language" that is meant to proclaim the mystery of Christ's *free, total, faithful,* and *fruitful* love. This is precisely what spouses commit to in marriage.

- Marital intercourse is meant to be a renewal of the marriage commitment itself expressed not with words, but with the language of the body.

- The body is "prophetic" because it is meant to proclaim the truth of God's love to the world. But we must be careful to distinguish true prophets from false prophets. If we can speak the truth with our bodies, we can also speak lies.

- All questions of sexual morality come down to one basic question: Is this act an authentic sign of God's *free, total, faithful, fruitful* love or is it not? If it is not, then it is a counterfeit to the love we really desire. We must be courageous enough not to settle for counterfeit "loves."

2. THE SACRAMENTAL SIGN OF MARRIAGE

Every sacrament has a specific sign (human dimension) that communicates the invisible reality of grace (divine dimension) it signifies.

- The sacramental sign of marriage is one of "manifold contents" (see TOB 105:6).

- It begins with the exchange of consent, is consummated in conjugal intercourse, and is borne in the spouses themselves throughout the duration of their marriage.

- The words of the wedding vows are consummated through the act of intercourse. Hence, if all of married life is a sacramental sign, we might say that marital intercourse is "the sign of that sign."

- Just as the body is the sign of the soul, the "one body" spouses become is the sign in some sense of the "soul" of their married life.

"THE CHURCH HAS BEEN ACCUSED OF BEING OBSESSED WITH SEX AND SEXUAL SINS, BUT THOSE WHO UNDERSTAND HOW CLOSE IS THE NEXUS BETWEEN SEX, LOVE, FAMILY, AND HUMAN HAPPINESS WILL REALIZE THE IMPORTANCE OF [JOHN PAUL II'S] MESSAGE."

– DR. JANET SMITH

2a. The exchange of consent 'is, of itself, only a sign of coming to be of marriage. And the coming to be of marriage is distinct from its consummation, so much so that without this consummation, marriage is not yet constituted in its full reality… In fact, the words themselves, 'I take you as my wife/husband,' do not only refer to be a determinative reality, but they can only be fulfilled bye thee *copula conjugale* (conjugal intercourse) … Thus, from the words with which the man and the woman express their readiness to become 'one flesh' according to the eternal truth established in the mystery of creation, we pass to the reality that corresponds to these words. Both the one and the other element are important with regard to the structure of the sacramental sign" (TOB 103:2-3).

2b. The "consent that binds the spouses to each other finds its fulfillment in the two 'becoming one flesh'" (CCC 1627).

2c. The marriage covenant "is the foundation of the union by which … 'the two will be one flesh' (Gen 2:24)." In this context "one can say that this bodily unity … is the regular *sign* of the communion of persons" (TOB 37:4).

3. The Body "Speaks"

All that John Paul has said about the body and its spousal meaning and about marriage as a "great mystery" imaging Christ's love for the Church is expressed and proclaimed through the "language of the body."

- The body "speaks" the deepest truth of man's existence as male and female. It not only speaks, but it "sings" – it sings the Song of Songs!

- The body speaks of man's call to love as God loves in a life-giving communion of persons. It speaks prophetically of God's love for humanity, Christ's love for the Church.

- God has given us the freedom to "author" the language of our own bodies. If we can speak the "truth" with the body, we can also speak "lies."

3a. Man "is constituted in such a way from the 'beginning' that the deepest words of the spirit – words of love, gift, and faithfulness – call for an appropriate 'language of the body.' And without this language, they cannot be fully expressed. We know from the gospel that this point applies both to marriage and to continence 'for the kingdom of heaven'" (TOB 104:7)

3b. "The body of each spouse will speak 'for' and 'on behalf of' each of them … carrying out the conjugal dialogue, which is proper to their vocation … The couple are called to form their lives and their living together as a 'communion of persons' on the basis of this language" (TOB 106:2).

3c. It "is the body itself that 'speaks'; it speaks with its masculinity or femininity … both in the language of faithfulness, that is, of love, and in the language of conjugal unfaithfulness, that is, of 'adultery'" (TOB 104:4).

So long as we are living the Sacrament as God designed

speak the truth or speak lies.

With our bodies

energy of the bond of conjugal union.

Profound intimacy

joy

Power of redemption

3d. For "every language ... the categories of truth and untruth (or falsity) are essential for it. In the text of the prophets ... *the body tells the truth* through faithfulness and conjugal love, and, when it commits 'adultery' it tells a lie, *it commits falsehood*" (TOB 104:8).

"Language of the Body" Reread in the Truth

"A 'prophet' is one who expresses with human words the truth that comes from God, one who speaks this truth in the place of God, in his name and in some sense with his authority" (TOB 105:2). Here the distinction between true from false prophets is critical (see TOB 106:4).

- Spouses marry "in the name of the Father, and of the Son, and of the Holy Spirit." In so doing, they pledge through their sacrament to proclaim the trinitarian language of their bodies faithfully.

- Joy and profound inner harmony come to married life only when the ongoing "dialogue" of the language of the body is honest – when spouses are "true prophets."

  > **3e.** "We can say that the essential element for marriage as a sacrament is the 'language of the body' reread in the truth. It is precisely through this that the sacramental sign is constituted" (TOB 104:9). "A correct rereading 'in the truth' is an indispensable condition for ... instituting the visible sign of marriage as a sacrament" (TOB 105:2).

  > **3f.** Spouses "are explicitly called to bear witness – by correctly using the 'language of the body' – to spousal and procreative love, *a testimony worthy of 'true prophets.'* In this consists the true significance and the greatness of conjugal consent in the sacrament of the Church" (TOB 106:4).

"Language of the Body" and the Battle with Lust

Is the "man of concupiscence" even capable of proclaiming "the whole depth of the Mystery of creation and redemption" in the context of marital intercourse? "With men this is impossible, but with God all things are possible" (Mt 19:26).

- John Paul is at pains, yet again, to proclaim the power of redemption to transform man's ethos, his heart, his orientation, his attitudes, his desires.

- Christ came "to restore the original order of creation disturbed by sin." Thus, Jesus "himself gives the strength and grace to live marriage" according to God's glorious intention (see CCC 1615).

> "THE ORGASM IS THE ACTUATION OF THE VITAL-CORPOREAL NATURE IN WHICH IT ATTAINS THE MAXIMUM INTENSITY OF WHICH IT IS CAPABLE, AND IN THE MERE QUALITY OF ITS BEING APPROACHES THE SPIRITUAL MOST CLOSELY ... DEATH IS THE GREATEST DIS-ACTUATION OF THE BODY – THEREFORE, IN ONE RESPECT THE OPPOSITE OF THE ORGASM."
>
> – DIETRICH VON HILDEBRAND

3g. "The analysis of Christ's words in the Sermon on the Mount leads us to understand … that the human 'heart' is not so much 'accused and condemned' by Christ because of concupiscence … but first of all 'called.' Here we find a decisive divergence between the anthropology of the Gospel and … the so-called masters of suspicion." Although "man naturally remains the man of concupiscence … he is at the same time *the man of the 'call.'* He is 'called' through the mystery of the redemption of the body" (TOB 107:1-2).

3h. While "concupiscence … brings about many 'errors' in rereading the 'language of the body' … nevertheless, in the sphere of the ethos of redemption there is always the possibility of passing from 'error' to the 'truth' … the possibility of … conversion from sin to chastity as an expression of a life according to the Spirit (see Gal 5:16)" (TOB 107:3).

Chastity is the virtue that unites eros & agape.

> "THE VERY EXPLOSIVENESS OF SEXUAL PLEASURE SUGGESTS THE GREATNESS OF THE CREATIVITY OF SEX. IN EACH CONJUGAL ACT, THERE SHOULD BE SOMETHING OF THE MAGNIFICENCE – OF THE SCOPE AND POWER – OF MICHELANGELO'S 'CREATION' IN THE SISTINE CHAPEL."
>
> – FATHER CORMAC BURKE

Summary

- Every sacrament has a specific sign (human dimension) that communicates the invisible reality of grace (divine dimension) it signifies. The sacramental sign of marriage begins with the exchange of consent, is consummated in conjugal intercourse, and is borne in the spouses themselves throughout the whole duration of their marriage.

- The deepest words of the spirit call for an appropriate "language of the body." In fact, the very words of the wedding vows can only be fulfilled by the marital embrace. Both the exchange of vows and their consummate expression in sexual intercourse are important with regard to the nature of the sacramental sign of marriage.

- Joy and profound inner harmony come to married life when the ongoing "dialogue" of the language of the body is honest. In fact, the essential element for marriage as a sacrament is learning to speak the "language of the body" in truth. The more *truthful* this language becomes, the more spouses prophetically proclaim God's mystery with their bodies.

- The distortions of concupiscence cause many errors in speaking the language of the body truthfully. Even so, through the gift of redemption, there is always the possibility of passing from *error* to the *truth*, of transforming lustful desire into loving desire.

STUDY QUESTIONS FOR:

SESSION 13: THE LANGUAGE OF THE BODY

1. Explain the relationship between wedding vows and sexual intercourse.

2. We have grown up in a culture that has almost entirely severed the link between sexual intercourse and marriage. What can I do to sure up this link in my mind and heart?

3. If a couple is sexually active before marriage and sees nothing wrong with it, what problems might this create when they do marry?

4. Imagine if the media understood and upheld the inherent link between sexual intercourse and wedding vows. What would our TV shows and movies look like?

5. Simply knowing in ones "head" that sexual intercourse is meant to express wedding vows is different than living this from the "heart." What practical steps can I take to make this journey from "head" to "heart"?

6. The *Catechism of the Catholic Church* says that Jesus himself gives the strength and grace to live marriage according to God's original design (see CCC 1615). That's a nice theory, but how can I live this in practice? How might this apply to unmarried people?

3/7/11

Session 14
SINGING THE SONG OF THE BODY

POINTS TO PONDER

Did you know that, of all the books in the Bible, the Song of Songs is at the center? Did you know that the Song of Songs is the favorite biblical book of the mystics? Did you know that saints have written more commentaries on this seemingly obscure and wildly erotic love poetry than on any other book in the Bible? What might the saints and mystics know that most Christians seem not to?

1. THE SONG OF SONGS

"All scripture is inspired by God and profitable for teaching, for reproof, for correction, and for training in righteousness" (2 Tim 3:16).

- Quoting from various scholars, John Paul seems critical of those who rush to disembody the Song of Songs, seeing it only as an allegory of God's "spiritual" love (see TOB 108, notes 95-96).

- He quotes one scholar who says that those who have "forgotten the lovers" or have "petrified them into pretense" do not interpret the Song correctly (see TOB 108, note 96).

- We needn't "ask forgiveness for the body." It is *not despite* the body and erotic love that we see God's mystery revealed in the Song, but precisely *in and through* these (see TOB 108, n. 96).

- The Song witnesses to a love that is simultaneously erotic *and* divine, spiritual *and* sensual (see TOB 111:5). They encounter spiritual realities by seeing, hearing, feeling, smelling, and even tasting each other (see Song 1:12-14; 2:3-6; 4:10-5:1).

    1a. Because the content of the Song of Songs is "apparently 'profane' … it [had] been placed among books forbidden to read." Yet, "it has been the source of the inspiration of the greatest mystical writers, and the verses of the Song of Songs have been inserted into the Church's liturgy" (TOB 108:2).

    1b. "What was barely expressed in the second Chapter of Genesis (vv. 23-25) in just a few simple and essential words is developed here in a full dialogue, or rather in a duet." Man's first words in Genesis "express wonder and admiration, or even better, the sense of fascination (see Gen 2:23). *And a similar fascination* … runs in fuller form through the verses of the Song of Songs" (TOB 108:5).

    1c. There mutual fascination is "concentrated on the 'body.'" In the integral view, attraction toward the body is *"attraction toward the other person … In addition, love unleashes a special experience of the beautiful,* which focuses on what is visible, although at the same time it involves the entire person. The experience of beauty gives rise to [mutual] pleasure" (TOB 108:6).

"My Sister, My Bride"

"You have ravished my heart, my sister, my bride, you have ravished my heart with one glance of your eyes … How sweet is your love, my sister, my bride!" (Song 4:9-10).

- Calling her "sister" *before* calling her "bride" has a "particular eloquence" (TOB 109:4). It shows that the man's desire for the woman is not one of lust but of love.

- He clearly sees her as a person who shares the same humanity. And when the term "sister" gives way to the term "bride," it does so without losing anything essential in the bridegroom's recognition of her as "sister."

   1d. Seeing his lover as a sister presents "a kind of challenge" for the man (TOB 109:4). The "bridegroom of the Song accepts the challenge … contained in the term 'sister'" (TOB 109:6).

   1e. "Through the [term] 'sister,' the bridegroom's words tend to reproduce … the history of the femininity of the beloved person; they see her still in the time of girlhood ('We have a little sister, and she still has no breasts') – and by means of this vision that goes back to the past, these words embrace her entire 'I,' soul and body, *with a disinterested tenderness*" (TOB 110:2).

"A Garden Closed, a Fountain Sealed"

You are "a garden enclosed, a fountain sealed" (Song 4:12).

- The Lover longs to enter this garden: "Open to me, my sister, my love, my dove, my perfect one; for my head is wet with dew" (Song 5:2). But he knows he cannot barge in or break down the door. Nor can he manipulate her into surrendering the key.

- He puts "his hand to the latch" (Sg 5:4) only with her freely given "yes." In total freedom (without any hint of coercion) she says: "I belong to my lover."

- If a person's "love" violates the one loved, then *it is not love* and should not be called love. It is love's counterfeit – lust.

   1f. "The bride appears to the eyes of the bridegroom as a 'garden closed' and 'fountain sealed' [because the] bride *presents herself to the eyes of the man as the master of her own mystery*. One can say that both metaphors … express the whole *personal dignity* … of that femininity which belongs to the personal structure of self-possession" (TOB 110:7).

   1g. Authentic love involves "initiation into the mystery of the person [without ever] implying the violation of that mystery" (TOB 111:1).

"FOR IN THIS BOOK, KISSES ARE MENTIONED, BREASTS ARE MENTIONED, CHEEKS ARE MENTIONED, LOINS ARE MENTIONED; AND THE HOLY PICTURES THESE WORDS PAINT ARE NOT MEANT FOR MOCKERY OR LAUGHTER … WE MUST [RATHER] NOTICE HOW MARVELOUSLY AND MERCIFULLY, IN MAKING MENTION OF THE PARTS OF THE BODY AND THUS SUMMONING US TO LOVE, [GOD] WORKS WITH US; FOR HE REACHES DOWN INTO THE VOCABULARY OF OUR SENSUAL LOVE IN ORDER TO SET OUR HEARTS ON FIRE, AIMING TO INCITE US TO A HOLY LOVING. INDEED, BY THE ACT IN WHICH HE LOWERS HIMSELF IN WORDS, HE ALSO ELEVATES OUR UNDERSTANDING; FOR FROM THE WORDS ASSOCIATED WITH THIS SENSUAL LOVE WE LEARN HOW FIERCELY WE ARE TO BURN WITH LOVE FOR THE DIVINE."

– POPE ST. GREGORY THE GREAT

2. WHEN THE "LANGUAGE OF THE BODY" BECOMES THE LANGUAGE OF THE LITURGY (REFLECTIONS ON TOBIT)

The Marriage of Tobias and Sarah

"You made Adam and gave him Eve his wife … And now, O Lord, I am not taking this sister of mine because of lust, but with sincerity. Grant that I may find mercy and grow old together with her. And [Sarah] said with him, 'Amen'" (Tb 8: 6-8).

- Tobias sets his heart on God's original plan for marriage. He calls her "sister." He contrasts lust with the sincere gift of self. He knows that he needs God's mercy to live the truth and he longs to spend his whole life with her.

- In receiving this mercy, they consummate their marriage and Tobias lives!

- In the face of authentic marital love, death has no chance. Life refuses to surrender! Their union joyously proclaims: "Where O death, is your victory? Where, O death, is your sting?" (1 Cor 15:55).

  2a. When spouses "unite as husband and wife, they … find themselves in the situation in which *the powers of good and evil fight against each other.*" The "choices and acts [of men and women] take on the whole weight of human existence in the union of the two" (TOB 115:2).

  2b. "Thus, from the very first moment, Tobias' love had *to face the test of life-or-death* … Tobias (and Sarah with him) go without hesitating toward this test." But in this test *"life has the victory* [because] during the test of the wedding night, love is revealed as stronger than death" (TOB 114:6).

  2c. "The truth and the strength of love show themselves in the ability to place oneself between the forces of good and evil that fight within man and around him, because love is confident in the victory of good and is ready to do everything in order that good may conquer" (TOB 115:2).

When the Language of the Liturgy Becomes the "Language of the Body"

With all that we've said about marriage as a sacramental participation in the "great mystery" of Jesus Christ, it shouldn't surprise us that John Paul speaks of conjugal life as being "liturgical."

- The Church celebrates her liturgy especially in and through the sacraments. Not only is conjugal life "liturgical," but the Church's liturgical life is in some sense "conjugal" (see CCC 1617).

- The one-flesh union is meant to be "eucharistic." Analogously, the Eucharist is the one-flesh union of Christ and the Church.

- The marital bed can be viewed as an altar upon which spouses offer their bodies in living sacrifice, holy and acceptable to God. This is their spiritual act of worship (see Rom 12:1; see also CCC 2031).

2d. Liturgy "means the participation of the People of God in 'the work of God'" (CCC 1069). It is the Church's "celebration of divine worship." The liturgy "involves the presentation of man's sanctification under the guise of signs perceptible by the senses and its accomplishment in ways appropriate to each of these signs" (CCC 1070).

2e. "The sacraments infuse holiness into the terrain of man's humanity: they penetrate the soul and body, the femininity and masculinity of the personal subject, with the power of holiness. All of this is expressed in the language of the liturgy … The liturgy … *elevates the conjugal covenant* of man and woman … *to the dimensions of the 'mystery,'* and at the same time enables that covenant to be realized in these dimensions through the 'language of the body'" (TOB 117b:2).

2f. "This seems to be *the integral meaning of the sacramental sign of marriage.* In this way, through the 'language of the body,' man and woman encounter the great *'mysterium'* in order to transfer the light of this mystery … into the 'language of the body' … On this road, conjugal life in some sense becomes liturgy" (TOB 117b:6).

> "CHRISTIAN MARRIAGE … IS IN ITSELF A LITURGICAL ACTION GLORIFYING GOD." AS A SACRAMENT, ITS "PURPOSE IS TO SANCTIFY GOD'S PEOPLE, TO BUILD UP THE BODY OF CHRIST, AND FINALLY, TO GIVE WORSHIP TO GOD."
>
> – POPE JOHN PAUL II

Summary

- The Song of Songs witnesses to a love that is simultaneously erotic *and* divine, spiritual *and* sensual. It is *not despite* the body and erotic love that we see God's mystery revealed in the Song, but precisely *in and through* these. Far from being "profane," the erotic poetry of the Song contains the mark of true holiness.

- To recognize his beloved first as "sister" before calling her "bride" demonstrates the sincerity of the lover's motives. He sees her as a person who shares his same humanity, not as an object for him to use and appropriate. The term "sister" challenges every man to approach woman with a disinterested (selfless) tenderness.

- The bridegroom sees his bride as a "garden closed" and "fountain sealed" because she presents herself to him as the "master of her own mystery." He longs to enter this garden, but she alone holds the key. Love *never* forces itself. Love leads the bridegroom into the mystery of the bride without ever violating that mystery.

- The story of Tobias and Sarah reveals that marriage is a "test of life-or-death." Love reveals itself to be stronger than death when it enters into the mystery of liturgy, of prayer, of God's mercy and grace which enables us to live marriage as God intended "in the beginning." Not only is conjugal life "liturgical," but the Church's liturgical life is also "conjugal."

STUDY QUESTIONS FOR:

SESSION 14: SINGING THE SONG OF THE BODY

1. How can the Song of Songs help us overcome any prejudice, fear, or suspicion that we might have towards sexuality and erotic love?

2. What effect do you think it might have on a relationship to skip the "fraternal theme" and jump immediately into romance and/or sexual activity?

3. Do you think it is more challenging for men to accept the "fraternal theme" of love than it is for women. If so, why? If not, why not?

4. Do the terms "sister" and "bride" ("brother" and "husband") seem to be in conflict in your mind? If so, reflect on the reason for that. Where, along the way of your own formation, did you come to believe that being "brother and sister" to each other was incompatible with being passionate lovers?

5. What personal ideas or attitudes might I need to address in order to recognize the compatibility of the terms "sister" and "bride"?

6. Explain in your own words what it means for a woman to be the "master of her own mystery." What happens to a woman's sense of self when she is not treated as such?

7. Explain in your own words what it means to say that marital love is "liturgical."

8. Is it odd or in any way "scandalous" for you to conceive of the marital embrace as something "liturgical," as an act of prayer and worship of God? If so, why?

9. What areas of my heart might be in need of healing to understand and (if married) to live sexual love as a profound prayer, as worship of God?

THE
LAW OF LIFE
IS OUR
Inheritance

May 23

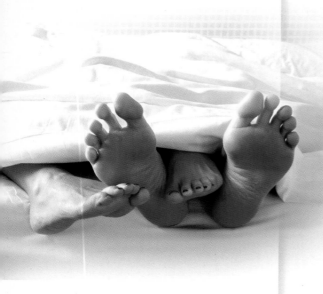

Session 15
The Teaching of *Humanae Vitae*

1. Review of Previous Series

Key points from Session Eight: *"The Language of Sexual Love"*

- The Church calls couples to a responsible exercise of parenthood. This could mean the generous and prudent decision to raise a large family or, because of a serious reasons to do otherwise, it could mean the decision to limit family size.

- The choice to *render* an act of intercourse sterile seriously violates the meaning of marital union as a sign of God's life-giving love. Abstaining from intercourse does not. In fact, abstaining from intercourse itself can be a profound act of love.

- Often times, love *demands* abstinence, and if one cannot abstain, his or her love is called in to question.

2. The Truth of the "Language of the Body"

Two Meanings of the Marital Act

The teaching of *Humanae Vitae* (HV) "is founded upon the inseparable connection, established by God which man on his own initiative may not break, between *the two meanings inherent to the conjugal act*: the unitive meaning and the procreative meaning" (HV 12).

- We can argue against contraception entirely from philosophy and natural law, but John Paul's catechesis shows the deepest *theological* reason for the immorality of contraception: it is a falsification of the sacramental sign of married love.

- Insert contraception into the language of the body and (knowingly or unknowingly) a couple engages in a *counter-sign* of the "great mystery."

- It's clear that attacking the unitive meaning of the act would violate the true meaning of love. What makes us think we can attack the procreative meaning of the act without violating love?

2a. This text of HV "is strictly linked with our earlier reflections about *marriage in the dimension of the (sacramental) sign.*" We "already said several times that this sign is based on the *'language of the body' reread in the truth* … Precisely *in this moment [the conjugal act], so rich in meaning*, it is also particularly important that the 'language of the body' be reread in the truth" (TOB 118:3,4).

2b. The language of the body has "clearcut meanings" (TOB 105:6) all of which are "'programmed' in a comprehensive way in conjugal consent" (TOB 106:3). For example, to "the question: 'Are you ready to accept children lovingly from God?' the man and the woman answer, 'Yes'" (TOB 105:6).

2c. When "the conjugal act is *deprived of its inner truth*, because it is deprived [willfully by the spouses] of its procreative capacity, it also *ceases to be an act of love*" (TOB 123:6).

2d. When the unitive and procreative meanings are willfully separated a "bodily union is brought about, but it does not correspond to the inner truth and to the dignity of personal communion … Such a violation of the inner order of conjugal communion … *constitutes the essential evil of the contraceptive act*" (TOB 123:7).

True Pastoral Concern

Paul VI expresses deep concern with the real problems and questions of modern man throughout HV. He states explicitly that he has no desire to pass over these problems and questions in silence (see HV 3).

- He acknowledges that some might find the encyclical's teaching "gravely difficult" if not "impossible to observe" (see HV 20).

- He states plainly, in fact, that men and women cannot live this teaching without the help of God's grace (see HV 20).

- Paul VI choice was either to trust in God's grace, or to compromise the truth. What is the truly loving, the truly "pastoral" thing to do?

  2e. "Pastoral concern means seeking the *true* good of man, promoting the values impressed by God in the human person; that is, it signifies applying the 'rule of understanding,' which aims at the ever clearer discovery of God's plan for human love, in the certainty that the *one and only true good* of the human person consists in putting this divine plan into practice" (TOB 120:6).

  2f. "To diminish in no way the saving teaching of Christ constitutes an eminent form of charity for souls" (HV 29).

3. Ethical Regulation of Fertility

The Primacy of Virtue

How can spouses avoid a pregnancy while respecting the true "language of the body"?

- If couples choose to "speak" the language of the body, they must do so honestly. But couples are not always obligated to speak.

- There is a vast difference between telling a lie and remaining silent. In fact, love often *demands* that couples "remain silent," that is, *abstain* from the marital embrace.

- In order to accord with the integral teaching of HV, continence must be practiced not merely as a "technique" for avoiding the conception of a child, but as a *virtue* that flows from reverence for the language of the body and from that interior "freedom of the gift."

- Just as spouses can engage in sexual union for the wrong reasons, they can also abstain for the wrong reasons.

  3a. *"As regards the immediate motivation, Humanae Vitae requires that 'in order to space births there must be serious reasons that stem either from the physical or psychological condition of the couple or from external circumstances' (HV 16)"* (TOB 124:5).

  3b. "For just reasons, spouses may wish to space the births of their children. It is their duty to make certain that their desire is not motivated by selfishness but is in conformity with the generosity appropriate to responsible parenthood" (CCC 2368).

  3c. "The parents themselves and no one else should ultimately make this judgements in the sight of God" (GS 50). This point is "of particular importance in determining ... *the moral character of 'responsible fatherhood and motherhood"* (TOB 121:2).

The Body Expresses the Person

HV is often accused of "biologizing ethics," that is, of reducing ethics to biology (see the work of Charles Curran). We "violate" or at least "interrupt" biological laws all the time (anesthesia, surgery, or even a hair cut). What's wrong with interrupting the biological process of fertility?

- HV stands as a constant reminder that "biological laws ... involve human personality" (HV 10).

- "Sexuality ... is by no means something purely biological, but concerns the inner-most being of the human person" (FC 11).

- We do no wrong when we "interrupt" biological processes for a greater good. But is the pleasure of an orgasm a greater good than a new human life?

    3d. "In the common way of thinking, it often happens that the 'method' [of natural birth regulation] is applied in a merely functional and even utilitarian, way." When this happens "one no longer sees the difference between it and other 'methods' … and one ends up speaking about it as if it were just another form of contraception" (TOB 125:4).

    3e. The difference between contraception and periodic abstinence "is much wider and deeper than is usually thought, one which involves in the final analysis two irreconcilable concepts of the human person and of human sexuality" (FC 32).

Our ears are designed to hear. Our eyes are designed to see. If someone went to a doctor and asked for a pill or a surgery to render his ears deaf or his eyes blind, one would rightly think he's out of his mind. And no doctor in *his* right mind would ever harm a person in such a way. To do so, in fact, would violate the Hippocratic oath – a doctor's traditional vow never to act *against* the health and functionality of the human organism. Continuing with the above line of reason, our genitals are designed to generate. When did we come to see our fertility as a disease that needs to be eliminated with devices, pills, and surgeries? And when did the medical profession stop professing the Hippocratic oath? Soon after the debut of the pill. It seems that rendering the female genitals sterile has since become their prescription of choice.

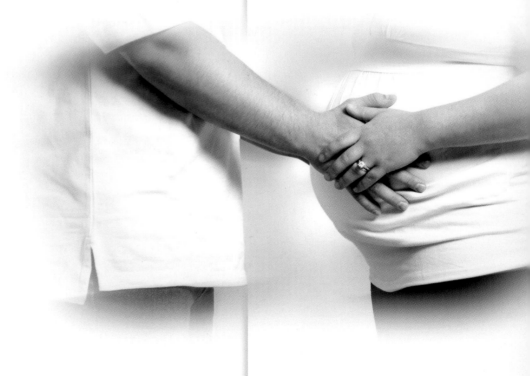

Summary

- The teaching of *Humanae Vitae* (HV) is founded upon the inseparable connection between the unitive and procreative meanings of the conjugal act. To attack one is to attack the other. Hence, a contracepted act of intercourse ceases to be an act of love. A physical union still takes place, but it is no longer a communion of persons in their body-soul integrity.

- The language of sexual intercourse has clear cut meanings, including openness to new life. Abstaining from intercourse is the only way to avoid a child that respects this language. However, such abstinence must be practiced not merely as a "technique" for avoiding a child, but as a *virtue* that flows from reverence for the sacramental sign of marriage.

- HV is often accused of reducing ethics to biology. But sexuality is by no means something merely biological. It concerns the inner-most being of the human person. Hence, HV is a constant reminder that biological laws involve the human person.

- When NFP is viewed in a merely functional way, one ends up speaking about it as if it were just another form of contraception. The true difference, however, between contraception and periodic abstinence involves two irreconcilable concepts of the human person and of human sexuality.

STUDY QUESTIONS FOR:

SESSION 15: THE TEACHING OF *HUMANAE VITAE*

1. John Paul II says that his reflections on *Humanae Vitae* are closely linked with our previous reflections on the sacramental sign of marriage. How so?

2. In his comic radio show, Garrison Keillor once summarized Catholic teaching on contraception as follows: "If you don't want to go to Minneapolis, what are you doing on the train?" How does this explain the Church's teaching?

3. Why does *each and every* act of intercourse have to remain ordained in itself towards the conception of a child? Isn't it sufficient to have the appropriate number of children and then enjoy the "care free" pleasures of sterilized sex?

4. In what way does a contracepted act of intercourse contradict the true meaning of love?

5. How does the Church's teaching against contraception safeguard the body-soul integrity of the human being?

6. What is the difference between abstaining from sex to avoid a child and rendering the sexual act sterile?

7. Why is the Church so "hung up" on all of this stuff?

1. THE POWER TO LIVE THE TRUTH OF LOVE

"The Church, while teaching [the] demands of the divine law, also announces the good news of salvation, and by means of the sacraments flings wide open the channels of grace, which makes man a new creature, capable of following the design of his Creator … with love and true freedom, finding the yoke of Christ to be sweet." By "the sacrament of Marriage, *spouses are strengthened and as it were consecrated* for the faithful … carrying out of their vocation even to perfection" (HV 25).

- HV responds basically to a single question: Is it possible for spouses to *love as God loves*? HV unhesitatingly proclaims, "Yes, it is!" But not on our own strength.

- In HV, Paul VI showed his confidence in the "power" of God poured into the hearts of spouses. To open to this power and live from it is to live an authentic "marital spirituality."

    1a. Education in "the theology of the body … constitutes already by itself the essential core of conjugal spirituality" (TOB 126:2).

    1b. "While *the powers of concupiscence* tend to *detach* the 'language of the body' from the truth, … *the power of love… strengthens it* ever anew in that truth, so that the mystery of the redemption of the body can bear fruit in it." Authentic marital love is "actively oriented … toward every true good. And thus its task consists in safeguarding the inseparable unity of the 'two meanings of the conjugal act'" (TOB 127:2).

Infallible and Indispensable Means

John Paul II speaks of three "*infallible and indispensable*" means for receiving the power to love (see TOB 126:5). These apply to anyone who wants to live the TOB, regardless of his or her state in life.

1. We must implore God for the power to love in **prayer**.

2. We must draw grace and love from the ever-living fountain of the **Eucharist**.

3. With humble perseverance, we must overcome our sins and faults in the sacrament of **Penance**.

1c. "'God's love has been poured out in our hearts by the Holy Spirit, who has been given to us' (Ro 5:5). This, then, is the essential and fundamental 'power' [to live as God intends]: *the love planted in the heart … by the Holy Spirit.*" Through prayer and the sacraments "that essential and *creative spiritual 'power' of love* reaches human hearts and, at the same time, human bodies" (TOB 126:5).

1d. "The great mystical tradition of the Church … shows how prayer can progress, as a genuine dialogue of love, to the point of rendering the person wholly possessed by the divine Beloved, vibrating at the Spirit's touch, resting filially [as a son or daughter] within the Father's heart. This is … a journey totally sustained by grace, which nonetheless demands an intense spiritual commitment and is no stranger to painful purifications (the 'dark night'). But it leads, in various possible ways, to the ineffable joy experienced by the mystics as 'nuptial union.' How can we forget here, among the many shining examples, the teachings of St. John of the Cross and St. Teresa of Avila?" (NMI 33).

1e. "*The Eucharist is the … sacrament of the Bridegroom and of the Bride.*" Christ, "in instituting the Eucharist … thereby wished to express the relationship between man and woman, between what is 'feminine' and what is 'masculine.' It is a relationship willed by God in both the mystery of creation and in the mystery of Redemption" (MD 26).

1f. "Without being strictly necessary, confession of everyday faults (venial sins) is nevertheless strongly recommended by the Church. Indeed the regular confession of our venial sins helps us form our conscience, fight against evil tendencies, let ourselves be healed by Christ and progress in the life of the Spirit" (CCC 1458).

In light of John Paul II's papal motto – *Totus Tuus* (I'm totally yours, Mary) – we can add a fourth "infallible" means for living the theology of the body: We must entrust the *entirety* of our lives to be formed in **Mary**, where Christ himself was formed.

1g. "A sculptor has two ways of making a statue. He may carve it … [or] he may cast it in a mold. An unhappy blow of the hammer or a slip of the chisel … may destroy the carver's work … Casting in a mold requires little work, little time, little expense. And if the mold be perfect … it forms the desired figure quickly, easily, and gently – provided the material used does not resist the operation. Mary, the great and unique mold of God, was made by the Holy Spirit to form the God-man, the man-God. In this mold, none of the features of the Godhead is missing. Therefore, whosoever is cast into it, and yields himself to the molding, receives all the features of Jesus Christ" (St. Louis deMontfort, *The Secret of Mary*).

"IN ITS ASCENT, LOVE, WITHOUT LOSING ORDER, LOSES MEASURE AND FINDS INTOXICATION."

– BLESSED JAN RUYSBROECK

"THERE ARE IN THIS EARTHLY PARADISE [OF MARY'S WOMB] UNTOLD RICHES, BEAUTIES, RARITIES, AND DELIGHTS … THERE ARE FLOWERBEDS … DIFFUSING A FRAGRANCE WHICH DELIGHTS EVEN THE ANGELS."

– ST. LOUIS DE MONTFORT

2. Analysis of the Virtue of Continence

Here "continence" refers to *the virtue* that makes man *truly free* in his ability to desire and to choose the good in thought and action. Here our previous reflections on "ethic" and "ethos" are decisive.

2a. "The difficulty [of living the teaching of HV] derives from the fact that *the power of love is planted in man threatened by concupiscence.*" Love "is not able to realize itself … except through mastery over concupiscence" (TOB 127:4).

2b. Each person "must devote himself to a progressive education in self-control of the will, of sentiments, of emotions, which must be developed from the simplest gestures, in which it is relatively easy to put the inner decision into practice" (TOB 128:1).

2c. "Self-mastery is a *long and exacting work.* One can never consider it acquired once and for all. It presupposes renewed effort at all stages of life" (CCC 2342).

2d. "The conviction that *the virtue of continence* 'opposes' the concupiscence of the flesh is correct, but it is not entirely complete" (TOB 128:2). "Continence is not only – nor even mainly – *the ability to 'abstain'* … this sort of function can be defined as 'negative.' But there exist also another function of self-mastery (which we can call 'positive'), and it is *the ability to orient* the respective *reactions* [of arousal and emotion], both as to their content and as to their character" (TOB 129:5).

2e. "If conjugal chastity (and chastity in general) manifests itself at first as an ability to resist the concupiscence of the flesh, it subsequently reveals itself as a *singular ability* to perceive, love, and realize those meanings of the 'language of the body' that remain completely unknown to concupiscence itself" (TOB 128:3).

2f. The sacrifice required "of continence … *does not impoverish … manifestations [of affection]*, but, on the contrary, it makes them spiritually more intense and thus *enriches* them" (TOB 128:3).

2g. "It is often thought that continence causes inner tensions from which men and women should free themselves. In the light of [our] analyses … continence, integrally understood, is, on the contrary, the one and only *way to free oneself from such tensions*" (TOB 129:1).

The Gift of Reverence

"Chastity means living in the order of the heart" (TOB 131:1). It is not only a moral virtue, it is also *a gift of the Holy Spirit* who fills us with profound "reverence" for what comes from God. St. Paul had this gift in mind when he exhorted spouses to "submit to one another out of reverence for Christ" (Eph 5:21).

Points to Ponder:

In the final analysis, contraception was not invented to prevent pregnancy. We already had a 100% safe and 100% reliable way of doing that. It's called abstinence. Why do we spay and neuter our dogs and cats? Why don't we just ask them to abstain? What are we doing to our dignity as free persons when we spay and neuter ourselves?

2h. "At the center of conjugal spirituality, therefore, stands chastity … as a virtue connected with the gifts of the Holy Spirit – *above all with the gift of reverence*." In becoming one flesh, spouses "cannot realize [the truth of] such a union … *except through the powers that come … from the Holy Spirit* who purifies, enlivens, strengthens, and perfects the powers of the human spirit" (TOB 131:2,3).

2i. The "gift of reverence for what is sacred" leads couples to be "full of veneration for *the essential values of conjugal union*" (TOB 131:4, 5). The conjugal union should express "veneration for the majesty of the Creator … and for the spousal love of the Redeemer" (TOB 132:3).

2j. "The attitude of *reverence for the work of God*, which the Spirit stirs up in the spouses, has an enormous *significance* for those … 'manifestations [of affection]' because it goes hand in hand with the capacity for profound pleasure in, admiration for, [and] disinterested attention to the … beauty of femininity and masculinity" (TOB 132:4).

2k. Concupiscence is "directed toward the other … as an object of enjoyment. Reverence for what God has created frees one from this constraint" and leads to "that 'deep-rooted peace' which is in some way the inner resonance of chastity" (TOB 132:3,5).

2l. The gifts of the Holy Spirit "initiate man and woman particularly deeply into reverence for the two inseparable meanings of the conjugal act … The gift of reverence … manifests itself also as a salvific fear … of violating or degrading what bears in itself the sign of the divine mystery of creation and redemption" (TOB 131:5).

2m. The "gift of reverence for what comes from God shapes the spirituality of the spouses *for the sake of protecting the particular dignity of [the conjugal] act*." It "guides one to understand, among the possible 'manifestations of affection,' the singular, and even exceptional, meaning of [the conjugal] act" (TOB 132:2).

2n. "Therefore, the antithesis of conjugal spirituality is constituted in some sense, by the subjective lack of … understanding [of the exceptional significance of the conjugal act] connected with anti-conceptive practices and mentality" (TOB 132:2).

"WE NEED TO RECOGNIZE THAT ANY FRUSTRATION WE FEEL IN THE PROCESS OF DOING NFP IS A SIGN THAT NFP *IS WORKING*. WHEN WE FEEL THOSE PAINS, WE MUST LEARN TO RECOGNIZE THEM AS THE GROWING PAINS THAT ACCOMPANY BOTH OUR ADVANCING SPIRITUAL MATURITY AND OUR INCREASING CAPACITY FOR TRUE LOVE (I.E., THE ABILITY TO WORK FOR THE GOOD OF THE OTHER EVEN WHEN DOING SO MAKES US UNCOMFORTABLE). IN THOSE TIMES WHEN THE GROWING PAINS – THE DISORDERED SEXUAL FRUSTRATION – HURT THE MOST, WE MUST RECOGNIZE THAT WE ARE NOT FEELING A SEXUAL URGE THAT MUST BE SATISFIED, BUT FEELING A SELFISH URGE THAT MUST BE CONTAINED AND TRANSFORMED. IN RESPONSE, WE MUST DRAW CLOSER TO OUR MATE, IN CONVERSATION, PRAYER, WORK, AND NONSEXUAL AFFECTION, AS A WAY OF RECLAIMING THE FREEDOM THAT OUR FALLENNESS HAS TAKEN FROM US."

– DR. GREGORY POPCAK

Summary

- HV responds basically to a single question: Is it possible for spouses to *love as God loves*? The Church unhesitatingly proclaims that it is – but not on our own strength. Through an authentic "marital spirituality," spouses must open their lives to the power of God. Education in the TOB already constitutes the essential core of marital spirituality.

- John Paul II speaks of three *"infallible and indispensable"* means for living the TOB: (1) We must implore God for the power to love in *prayer*; (2) We must draw grace and love from the *Eucharist*; (3) With humble perseverance, we must overcome our sins and faults in the sacrament of *Penance*. A true devotion/entrustment to Mary is also critical.

- It is the pull of concupiscence that explains the difficulty of living the TOB. Love is not possible except through mastery over concupiscence. If chastity manifests itself at first as an ability to resist concupiscence, it gradually reveals itself as the singular ability to experience a depth of love and joy that remains completely unknown to concupiscence.

- Chastity lies at the very center of an authentic marital spirituality. As a virtue, it demands human effort, but it is also a gift of the Holy Spirit. It is not possible for spouses to realize the truth of their sexual union except through the powers that come from the Holy Spirit who purifies, enlivens, strengthens, and perfects the powers of the human spirit.

- The Holy Spirit's gift of reverence fills spouses with a deep-felt need to safeguard the profound dignity and exceptional meaning of the conjugal act, whatever the cost. Therefore, the antithesis of conjugal spirituality is constituted in some sense by the lack of reverence manifested by contraceptive practice and the contraceptive mentality.

STUDY QUESTIONS FOR:

SESSION 16: OUTLINE OF MARITAL SPIRITUALITY

1. Explain in your own words what is meant by "marital spirituality." What does this have to do with contraception?

2. Pope Paul VI said that in proclaiming the fullness of the divine law, at the same time the Church also "flings wide open the channels of grace." Why are both elements – the fullness of the law and the power of grace – essential in understanding the Church's teaching in HV?

3. Many people object that the abstinence required in practicing NFP prevents a couple from expressing their love for one another. Explain the fallacy in this way of thinking.

4. Many people (if not most) consider chastity a big "no" to sex. It is true that chastity demands saying no to lust, but John Paul II highlights another *entirely positive* dimension of chastity. What is it?

5. How can we distinguish between a spiritually mature sexual desire that is filled with the passion to love (as Christ loves) and sexual desire that is filled with the passion of lust?

6. John Paul II says that it is "the concupiscence of the flesh" that makes it difficult to appreciate and practice the teaching of HV. Explain what he means.

7. How is the divine gift of reverence related to the virtue of chastity?

8. John Paul II used very strong language when he described the practice of willfully sterilizing sex as "the antithesis" of an authentic marital spirituality. Do you think this language is justified? Why or why not?

Glossary

Adequate anthropology: A full and integral understanding of what it means to be human.

Communion of persons: Refers to the unity or "common union" established when persons mutually give and receive "the sincere gift of self." The male-female communion of persons in marriage is a created image of *the* Communion of Persons found in the Trinity.

Divine mystery: Refers to the two-fold "inner secret" of God: first, that God exists as a Trinity of persons in an eternal "exchange of love," and, second, that God has destined man (male and female) to participate in this exchange of love.

Embodied spirit: Refers to man as a person in the unity of his body and spirit.

Eros (Greek for sexual love) and *agape* (Greek for divine love): Christ's love is *free, total, faithful,* and *fruitful.* In Christian marriage, *eros* and *agape* are called to meet and bear fruit. If spouses are to be faithful to the "language of their bodies," sexual intercourse must express *agape*.

Ethic and *ethos*: An *ethic* is an objective moral law or command. *Ethos*, on the other hand, refers to the abiding inner desires of the heart—what attracts and repulses a person. In the Sermon on the Mount, Christ demonstrates that the ethic is not enough ("You have heard the command … but I tell you … "). Christ came to transform our *ethos*, i.e., to change our hearts.

Eunuch: Someone physically incapable of sexual intercourse. A *eunuch for the kingdom* is someone who chooses freely to forgo sexual intercourse in order to devote himself or herself totally to the "marriage of the Lamb" (i.e., the eternal union of Christ and the Church).

Every-day mystic: Men and women who have caught the "fire" that Christ came to cast on the earth. Through all of life's joys and trials, the every-day mystic senses God's loving plan unfolding and abandons himself or herself to it with loving trust.

Gift: Refers to God's self-giving in creation. God initiates His self-gift by creating us in His image. We re-present that gift by living in the image in which we're made.

Freedom of the Gift: Refers to freely giving and receiving the gift of one person to another, rather than grasping at or desiring to possess the other.

Gift of God: God's true disposition is one of self-donation ("gift"). God's gift to man is participation in His own divine life.

Icon: In general, a sign or likeness that stands for an object by signifying or representing it. As it relates to the Theology of the Body, the body is an icon of God's mystery of love.

Idol: An object or activity that is worshipped in place of God.

Incarnation: The doctrine that refers to the Eternal Word, the second Person of the Holy Trinity, taking on human flesh and being born of a woman.

Interpretation of suspicion: As applied to sexual matters, a view that cannot imagine any prism other than lust through which to see, live, and understand sexuality.

Sacrament of redemption: Refers to the "sign" that makes the mystery of redemption visible. That sign is the "spousal union" of Christ and the Church consummated in the Eucharist.

Knowledge: Refers to the deepest essence of the reality of shared married life.

Language of the Liturgy: The liturgical life of the Church is her celebration of the "great mystery" of Christ's love for the Church primarily through prayer and the sacraments, especially the Mass. For spouses to live marriage as it was meant to be, they must allow their love to be taken up in the Church's liturgy. Spousal love must become "liturgical."

Language of the body: Refers to the body's capacity to "speak" or "proclaim" God's love. It does so — or is meant to do so—most profoundly in the "one flesh" union of spouses. Here, spouses are meant to renew their marriage vows with their bodies.

Life in the Spirit: One who has allowed himself to be "possessed" by the love of God, readily following the promptings of God, lives a life "according to the Spirit." The Holy Spirit empowers spouses to live the Christian ethos of marriage. Life in the Spirit "allows man and woman to find again the true freedom of the gift together with the awareness of the spousal meaning of the body" (TOB 101:1,4)

Lust: Refers to sexual desire void of God's love. Lust leads a person toward *self-gratification* at the expense of the other, while love leads a person toward *self-donation* for the good of the other. Lust, therefore, is a *reduction* of the original fullness God intended for the sexual relationship.

Manichaeism: The heresy that sees the source of evil in matter and therefore condemns all that is bodily in man, especially sex.

Mystical marriage: The "great mystery" of Christ's spousal union with the Church in which we are all called to participate as human beings.

Naked without shame (original nakedness): Adam and Eve were untainted by shame because they had no experience whatsoever of lust. Before sin, man and woman experienced sexual desire as the desire to love in God's image.

Primordial sacrament: John Paul II called marriage the "primordial sacrament" because it refers right from the beginning to the "great mystery" of Christ's union with the Church.

Purity of heart: To the degree that we are pure of heart we understand, see, and experience the body as God created it to be, as a revelation of his own divine mystery. "Blessed are the pure in heart, for they shall see God" (Matthew 5:8).

Redemption of the body: The restoration of the human person in his or her integrity as a unity of body and soul. It affords the recovery of God's original plan in the human heart. This redemption is not only something we hope for in the resurrection from the dead, it is already at work in us within history.

Resurrection of the body: The doctrine that the human body is also destined for everlasting life in union with the human soul. Eternal life is not only a "spiritual" reality. Man (male and female) is destined to share in the life of the Trinity as a body-person.

Reverence: Refers to the sense of awe that fills a person in the presence of the holy. Reverence for the body and for the "great mystery" of sexuality is the surest foundation for chastity.

Sacrament: In its more ancient meaning, this refers to a physical sign that makes visible what is invisible. In its more strict meaning, sacrament refers to the seven signs of the new covenant (i.e., baptism, confirmation, Eucharist, penance, anointing of the sick, holy orders, and marriage) instituted by Christ to confer the grace of redemption.

Sacramentality of the body: Refers to the body's capacity of making visible what is invisible. The body proclaims a "great mystery" — the spiritual mystery of God's Trinitarian love and our call to share in that love through Christ.

Shame: In its negative sense, shame indicates that we have lost sight of the dignity and goodness of the body as a "theology" — a revelation of God's mystery. In its positive sense, shame indicates a desire to protect the goodness of the body from the degradation of lust.

Spiritualized body: Refers to the fact that the human body is "in breathed" not only with a spiritual soul but also, through the grace of redemption, with God's Holy Spirit.

Spousal analogy: The biblical use of marital love as an earthly image of God's love for Israel and, in the New Testament, Christ's love for the Church. Like all analogies, the spousal analogy is inadequate in communicating God's infinitely transcendent mystery. Yet, according to John Paul II, it is the most fitting human image of the divine mystery.

Spousal meaning of the body: The call to love as God loves inscribed in the human body as male and female. If we live according to the spousal meaning of our bodies, we fulfill the very meaning of our being and existence

The heart: Our deepest interior self where we are "alone" with ourselves and with God. It is here that we experience the battle between good and evil, where sin wounds us, and where Christ meets us and heals us.

Theology of the body: The study of how God reveals his mystery through the human body. This is also the title of John Paul II's 129 short talks on the subject.

ABOUT CHRISTOPHER WEST

Christopher West is recognized around the globe for his work promoting an integral, biblical vision of human life, love, and sexuality. He serves as a research fellow and faculty member of the Theology of the Body Institute near Philadelphia, Pennsylvania. He has also lectured on a number of other prestigious faculties, offering graduate and undergraduate courses at St. John Vianney Seminary in Denver, the John Paul II Institute in Melbourne, Australia, and the Institute for Priestly Formation at Creighton University in Omaha.

Christopher is the best-selling author of several books and one of the most sought after speakers in the Church today. He and his wife, Wendy, live with their five children near Lancaster, Pennsylvania.

OTHER RESOURCES BY CHRISTOPHER WEST

Books

Good News About Sex and Marriage: Answers to Your Honest Questions about Catholic Teaching (Servant, 2000)

Theology of the Body Explained: A Commentary on John Paul II's "Man and Woman He Created Them" (Pauline, 2003; revised edition, 2007)

Theology of the Body for Beginners: A Basic Introduction to John Paul II's Sexual Revolution (Ascension Press, 2004)

The Love That Satisfies: Reflections on Eros and Agape (Ascension Press, 2007)

Heaven's Song: Sexual Love as it was Meant to Be (Ascension Press, 2008)

Audio and Video Productions

Ascension Press is Christopher West's official publisher of audio and video presentations, including *The Gift* series. For more information, visit *AscensionPress.com* or *TheologyoftheBody.com* or call 1-800-376-0520.

Speaking Engagements

To schedule a speaking engagement by Christopher West, visit *ChristopherWest.com* and click on the "speaking" link.

Coming Soon...

Look for more <u>specialized</u> studies such as *Men's, Women's, Marriage Enrichment, Young Adult*, and more. If you have questions about any of our Theology of the Body products or about how to implement *The Gift* study system, please call 1-800-376-0520 or visit www. AscensionPress.com.